Beckwith West

Experience of a Confederate States prisoner

Beckwith West

Experience of a Confederate States prisoner

ISBN/EAN: 9783744785648

Printed in Europe, USA, Canada, Australia, Japan

Cover: Foto ©Andreas Hilbeck / pixelio.de

More available books at **www.hansebooks.com**

EXPERIENCE

OF A

Confederate States Prisoner,

BEING

AN EPHEMERIS

REGULARLY KEPT BY

An Officer of the Confederate States Army.

RICHMOND:

WEST & JOHNSTON, PUBLISHERS.

1862.

G. W. GARY, PRINTER.

PREFACE.

The gallant Morgan has said that our independence is an achieved fact. "Privation and suffering have won it." It is true that the noble South has been deprived of many of its wonted necessaries, not to say luxuries, by the present invasion of those disciples of Satan, commonly called "Yankees." Paper, among other things, is scarce in the South, and paper may be turned into excellent account in the composition of cartridges, while metal that might be moulded into bullets is run into type. Yet newspapers and books are printed, and most of them eagerly read, especially any that have the most remote bearing upon the present contest. In these stern times of war's realities, plain facts challenge our attention rather than the gaudy fiction of novels. Honey from Mount Hybla, or Nectar from Olympus, would fail on the palate, unless relieved by homelier viands; and it would certainly require considerable stoicism to sit down to a tale of imaginary woes and sorrows while one great wail is going up from our sick and wounded—an incredible amount of apathy to sit leisurely down to such a book under the shade of a tree while the nation is sending out a heartcry for reinforcements to our brave legions, in order to *speedily* defeat the unscrupulous enemy. This little book is intended as, and professes no more than a plain statement of facts, so that others may learn what I have read, seen and heard, without undergoing the pain of incarceration in the hands of Yankees, whose tyranny increases in proportion to the power they possess over their victims.

EXPERIENCE

OF A

CONFEDERATE STATES PRISONER.

May, 1862. A "heavy march" on the 6th and 7th instant resulted in a Confederate victory at McDowell, Highland county, at which place a battle was fought on the 8th. General Jackson routed and drove the enemy, commanded by the Yankee Generals, Milroy and Schenck, twenty-five miles into Pendleton county, and captured a large amount of ammunition, commissary stores, arms, and many prisoners. Our forces afterwards completely routed Banks' column at Winchester, and thoroughly defeated Fremont and Shields at Cross Keyes and Port Republic. After the battle at Front Royal, I remained at that place upon the recommendation of the regimental surgeon, on account of having strong symptoms of the Typhoid fever, which turned out to be the genuine disease. Dr. Brown, the resident physician, attended me ; and a member of my own company, Mr. Oxford, nursed me faithfully from the 23d May, the day our forces entered Front Royal, to the 30th May, the day that the Yankees under General Shields recaptured it. The 12th Georgia regiment was the only force left at Front Royal. The Provost Marshal, or the Colonel commanding the 12th Georgia, gave us notice but *one hour* before the Yankees were in the town that they were advancing. When Mr. Oxford informed me of the near approach of the Yankees, I quickly jumped out of bed, and we hastily made a retreat towards Winchester. The salutary and kind attentions of Dr. Brown and Mr. Oxford had much improved me in strength, but I soon discovered that I could not keep pace with the latter in our eager efforts to escape. We succeeded in getting about one mile and a half from the town when the Yankee cavalry were heard closing on us so fast that we leaped over a fence on the left of the road, thinking that we might conceal ourselves in the high grass until the cavalry passed, and be enabled to elude them by getting into the woods near by. In the confusion, however, Mr. Oxford and I became separated, and by this time the Yankee cavalry were close enough to fire twice on myself and two others from the 33d Virginia, who attempted to make their escape in the same direction. The cavalry soon after had surrounded us, and we were compelled to surrender, and were marched into town under a heavy guard The commissioned officers were carried before General Shields, and the non-commissioned officers and privates to the building used by our army as a hospital, where we had some hundred sick at the time. The commissioned officers at first confined to any house they might select, were afterwards paroled the town. I was taken to Mr. John B. Petty's house, and ordered to remain there " for the present" by one of General Shields' staff. About an hour after I was left at the above named house, a Pennsylvania Major came into the room where I was, and very abruptly asked me, "What are you doing here ?" I informed him that by order of General Shields I was to remain there "until further orders ;" he would not believe me, and placed *two* sentinels in the room until he found that my statement was correct. Captain Keogh (on General Shields' staff) gave me the following note, saying, when he did so, that I would not be "any further annoyed by officers in other regiments" that had nothing to do with my case :

"HEADQUARTERS, SHIELDS' DIVISION, MAY 30, 1862.

" Captain W. is allowed to remain at the house of Mr John B. Petty (until further arrangements are made,) the said Captain W, being a prisoner of war. By order of Major General Shields.

MILES W. KEOGH,
Ass't Adj."

After the lapse of two days I was allowed the limits of the town, but being sick I did not go out of the house for five days after I was captured, when I walked down to the barbers' shop. While passing the hotel I was called by a Federal officer, whose name I learned afterwards was General Duryea, of New York. I went into his room, around which were sitting several other Federal officers, and the General addressed me, " What are you doing walking about the streets ? Are you not a Southern officer ?" I replied " I am," and told him that Major Shedd, the Provost Marshal, had paroled me the town. General Duryea then said, " I understand, sir, that when the Rhode Island cavalry had you in their power, and could have killed you, that as one of the cavalry dismounted to take your sword, and was proceeding to mount again, you fired your pistol twice at the back of his neck." I replied such could not be true, for I had no pistol about me when captured. General Duryea then said, " I may be mistaken, but I wish to find out what Captain it was, and visit the proper vengeance upon him." The day before the Yankees entered Front Royal, a colored man died of small pox in a small frame house near the railroad depot, and by general consent of both citizens and the Yankee paroled prisoners in the town, it was agreed as advisable to burn the house and body, in order to prevent the spread of the dangerous and contagious disease. The Yankees were told by some traitor, or else themselves originated the lie, that we had burned up two of the Yankee prisoners in our hands, and they swore vengeance against us—declared that they intended to "put the town in ashes," and nothing but a special order of General Shields to the contrary, and forbidding interference with any property whatever, prevented the soldiers from giving vent to spleen engendered by a false and malicious report. General Shields was informed by Major Collins, (Vermont cavalry,) in my presence, that while a prisoner in our hands he was treated most kindly, and that all reports to the contrary had no foundation in truth ; and all the other Federal prisoners endorsed the statement of Major Collins.

June 6th. We have been told from day to day that all " General Jackson's men" would be paroled until exchanged, and yet at the same time preparations are being made to take us to Washington, *i. e.*, about nineteen officers, and one hundred and fifty non-commissioned officers and privates. The kindness of the people of Front Royal, and especially the ladies to the Confederate prisoners, deserves the highest praise. Devoted to our cause, they omit no opportunity to show their regard for those who are endeavoring to rescue them from the obnoxious presence and depredations of the Yankees. They keep aloof from the Yankees as much as possible, and are always on the alert to do something for the relief of our sick and wounded.

June 7th. Among the Yankees I made the acquaintance of Adjutant Griffin, 5th New York cavalry, who treated me kindly, as also Captain Abraham Moore, Captain Isaac S. Tichenor, and Major Shedd, 105th New York regiment, and Lieutenant H. Hobert Mason, of General McDowell's staff. Met with the celebrated Miss " Bell Boyd" to-day. Miss B. is a sprightly, intelligent lady, *au fait* in all the movements of our army, and moderately good looking. Her general information, and nonchalant mode of fluent conversation, renders her *tout ensemble* quite interesting. *It is said* she has obtained valuable information from Yankee officers in regard to their movements, and conveyed the same to our army. A great many soldiers talk to me every day, and they all so far have expressed themselves tired of the war, but say that it will soon be ended, inasmuch as they have General Jackson "in a trap," out of which he cannot escape. They say "Stonewall" is our greatest General—incomparably so—that he is cunning and strategetic, but that it is not within the range of human possibility for him " to clude us this time ;" that they would like to capture him, but under no consideration would they kill either him or Ashby if they knew it.

June 8th. They say we are to be sent to Washington city on to-morrow, but we have been told so many things that have failed to come to pass, that we are too reluctant to believe any more reports. *Nous verron;* to-morrow. Mr. and Mrs. Petty have been untiring in their attentions to the sick and wounded prisoners here. They will never be forgotten by those who have been the recipients of their kindness, especially those who had the fortune to be under their roof. Mr. P has been made to pay the Yankees a heavy penalty on account of being " Secesh ;" they have stolen three of his most valuable negroes, any number of horses, cattle, &c., besides laying waste his two farms. One of his negro men left him one day, and the next time he saw him the negro was dressed in the cavalry uniform, with a sabre hanging to his side, and passed his master with silent contempt on the street. The negro was now a member of the " Michigan cavalry," a company notorious for its success in robbery and plunder of every description. This same negro visited Mr. Petty's house afterwards in company with three Yankee officers, and demanded of Mrs. Petty (Mr. P. was absent) the key to the wine room ; Mrs. P told them that she had only a few bottles of wine, which she kept for medicinal purposes, and requested them not to disturb it, but the negro persisted with threats in having it, and told Mrs. P. " she lied" in saying she only had a few bottles. Having obtained all the wine in the house, by freightening this excellent lady they drank it in her presence, when they smashed the bottles on the floor, exclaiming, " the damned Secesh don't deserve to have anything."

Monday, June 9th. To-day the prisoners were put on the cars to be taken to Washington city. A lady gave one of the prisoners a boquet with a small Confederate flag attached, which, as he was about to get into the cars, was noticed by General Duryea, of New York, and as soon as the latter saw it he quickly severed the flag from the boquet, and with an air of contempt and triumph tore it into fragments, at the same time trampling each fragment under his feet. The people of Front Royal manifest the greatest interest in the Confederate prisoners. They carry provisions to them daily at the hospital, while those prisoners who are paroled are invited to their houses. It would seem that interest would sometimes prompt them to court Yankee favor, but they spurn it, and remain loyal and true in their deportment at the sacrifice of thousands of dollars worth of property, for Yankee regiments camp on the wheat fields, and steal the horses and negroes, and kill the hogs, and commit every sort of depredation upon the property of those who are known to be Secessionists. The ladies avoid the Yankees whenever they can, and when thrown into their presence, treat them with that reserve with which they might be expected to treat those whom they regard as the deadly enemies of their dearest friends and interest, but whose presence they cannot avoid. The people seemed sad when the prisoners left Front Royal; the ladies filled their haversacks with refreshments, and loaded the cars with flowers.

June 10th. We arrived at Alexandria at 2 o'clock this morning—saw the depot which was burned by the bold General Geary, when he *imagined* that he saw 50,000 rebels advancing on him, when, in fact, the rebels were no where near him. The 104th New York regiment in their fright burned up everything they had. A fellow prisoner informs me that he was lately a prisoner in the hands of Geary, who had him hand-cuffed, and kept him without food for four days, and that he led his command to believe, by repeated assurances, that Richmond was in possession of the Federal army. At daybreak this morning a crowd assembled around the cars, and many were eager to talk with us, but were not permitted to do so. Nor were our friends allowed to give us anything to eat, although they had provided various refreshments, and although the Yankees had furnished us nothing to eat since yesterday morning, or it may be said with nothing at all, for what we eat *then* was given by the people at Front Royal. At 7 o'clock in the morning the crowd became very great, and the guards were increased in proportion. The ladies could not be prevented from kissing their hands to the prisoners. A young man attempted to throw an orange in the cars for a lady, who requested him to do so, but he was contemptuously thrust aside, and had to leave in "double quick" time. Our friends had provided for us coffee, bread and butter, ham, eggs, cakes, pies, candies in variety, and tobacco and cigars in profusion, but like the thirsty Tantalus, and the water we were almost in reach, without being able to enjoy them. Boquets were thrown in showers into the cars, while there was the greatest demand for our buttons. Some cut all the buttons off their coats, and then could not gratify all who requested to be

2

given "one." This scene, and the sympathy manifested for our
cause by so many Alexandrians, made us feel happy, while at
the same time we were sad in knowing that they were then
writhing under the heel of Lincoln despotism. The Yankee soldiers seemed to envy the attentions sought to be lavished upon
the prisoners by the people of Alexandria ; some cursed us,
some shook the United States flag in our faces, &c. One fellow
remarked, ."If the 11th Massachusetts was in those cars, you
would not get to Washington city " Others vented their spleen
by insulting remarks to the ladies. We arrived at Washington
at 12, M., having started from Alexandria in a steamboat about
11. We were then marched in two ranks (with a strong guard
of infantry on either side and rear, and a display of cavalry in
front) to the "old capitol military prison." We were very wet
when we arrived at the latter place, on account of the rain which
commenced before we left the steamboat, but were compelled to
stand out in the yard from 12, M., to 5, P M., when we were
assigned our quarters. The room in which seven officers and
myself were confined was about twelve feet square. My prison
companions are Captain Samuel M. Sommers, quartermaster,
Lieutenants Chas. E. Bott and John F Everly, 33d Virginia
regiment, and Lieutenant James K. Decrow, Newton T. John-
ston, James M. Brown, and Edward Waterman, of the 12th
Georgia regiment. Roll was called to-night, and our names,
rank, regiment, company letter, and State, taken in full. Our
door is locked all the time, except when officers come in, or when
we are allowed to go into the yard an half hour for exercise.

June 11th. The superintendent of this prison is William P
Wood, and the officers in command Captain Benjamin Higgins,
and Lieutenants J. Miller and ——— Holmes. Mr. Wood is an
infidel, who so far from blushing to proclaim it, takes frequent
occasion to do so. When endeavoring to enforce his doctrines,
he addresses his opponent as " You mullet-headed Christian,"
and speaks in the greatest derision of our Saviour, while he de-
nies the existence of a God, or hell. He is a sharp-featured,
serpentine-looking specimen of humanity, medium height, and
by trade a cabinet maker, before his black republican proclivities
secured him his present position. Mr. Wood, a prisoner, soon
finds out to be the most important among " the powers that be"
connected with the prison, and all " privileges" must be reached
through him. He professes to be a great Southern man, and
sometimes demonstrates this by knocking down a contraband,
who does not wait upon him in accordance with his fastidious
notions.

It is cloudy, and my close confinement, together with the con-

CONFEDERATE STATES PRISONER.

tinual sight of dark blue uniforms makes me feel as gloomy as
the sky is in appearance. I would that I could be with our army
in the "Old Dominion." From my prison window I see an old
United States soldier cultivating flowers in a row of flower pots.
One knows him to be a soldier by his regular walk, and the
style of his grey moustache, not to speak of his uniform. Indeed one might have guessed as much from the care he takes of
his little garden, for there are two things I have noticed especially, loved by old soldiers, viz : flowers and children. They
have so long been obliged to look upon the earth as a field of battle, and so long cut off from the peaceful pleasures of a quiet
lot, that they seem to begin life at an age when others end it.

June 12th. Have been here a day and a half and two nights,
and can form some idea of the way things are managed at this
prison. Roll is called night and morning, and as to fare, we are
allowed a tin cup of what is called coffee, but which is really
mock-coffee, a slice of bread six inches long, five inches wide, and
a quarter of an inch thick, and a piece of beef or fat bacon twice
a day—forming a repast, the sight of which is almost enough to
cause any respectable stomach to revolt, so unclean seems both
it and its surroundings. A lady came into our room to-day lean-
ing on the arm of Dr. Stewart, the prison surgeon. As the Doc-
tor ushered her in, he remarked, "This is the room in which
Mrs. Rose O. N. Greenhow was confined." Lieutenant D., of
the 12th Georgia regiment, was lying on a blanket in one corner
of the room, and the lady seemed to recognise him, and asked
"What's your name?" "Are you from Georgia?" Being answered promptly by the Lieutenant, and in the affirmative as to
the latter question, the surgeon observed, "You have a remarkable recollection of faces," and they left the room, which was
then quickly locked. It is supposed that she is the correspondent of some Northern journal. No doubt she will say that we
live in a palace, and have hotel fare, thus emulating the editor
of the "Evening Star," who a short time ago informed its read-
ers that we "fared equal to any hotel in the city." If a sentinel is caught in conversation with a prisoner, the punishment is
two weeks in chains. The prisoners are allowed an half hour in
the yard after each meal. After dinner to-day, the surgeon, Dr.
Stewart, a coarse, vulgar mean Yankee came among us in the
yard, and had the audacity to say, "All who desire to take the
oath of allegiance to the United States Government, and thereby obtain their liberty step this way." A deserter and two men
of Northern birth obeyed the call. I am informed by prisoners,
who have been here sometime, that the greatest effort is constantly made to induce prisoners to take the infamous "oath of

allegiance." At roll call to-night I was informed that "several friends" called to see me. I was not told who the friends are, and I infer that they do not intend to tell me, or allow me to see them at all.

Friday, June 13th. Among the prisoners confined here, is Charles C. Randolph, Esq., a venerable looking old gentleman, seventy-five years of age, from Fauquier county, Virginia. He served in the war of 1812 as Captain, under General Parks' command, and received his commission through the influence of the celebrated " Harry Lightfoot Lee," of the revolution. He says that he went to Richmond about the first of April last, and when he returned to his home he found that the Yankees had devastated everything about his valuable premises. They stole his horses, sheep and cattle, and destroyed his crops, and took everything of value he had from a library worth $5,000, to his bed, and even his wife's likeness, and the family bible, besides breaking all the hinges of the doors, and committing waste and robbery generally. He, himself, was arrested as soon as he arrived home, and brought here, for what he knows not, unless it be for implied sympathy for the cause of the soil of his birth and the people of his blood. There was a prisoner here named Wharton, a Californian. He was a Lieutenant in the United States Navy at the beginning of the war, when he resigned, and started for the South via Washington city, but was arrested on his arrival here and brought to this prison. A short time since he cursed one of the sentinels for insulting language used towards him, when the sentinel called for the " corporal of the guard," who being equally insolent, was in turn treated in the same way by Lieutenant Wharton. The " officer of the guard" was then called, who proving equally offensive in language to Lieutenant W., the latter cursed him in the heat of anger, whereupon said Lieutenant Wharton was shot, and soon afterwards died of his wounds. A respectable gentleman, Mr. Stewart of Maryland, who was incarcerated here, was promised by the guard to be allowed to escape, on condition of the payment of $50 ; but although the sentinel pocketed the money, when Mr. Stewart was effecting his escape the sentinel shot him, and this sentinel was immediately promoted from a private to a .sergeant.

Saturday, June 14th, 1862. It is reported this morning that Colonel Ashby is killed, and General " Stonewall" Jackson a prisoner, and the Yankees profess to place great reliance upon the report. From Northern sources, I learn that when the war-tax was being collected in Southern Illinois, it required three regiments to accomplish the task. It seems plain that Southern Illinois would like to break the chains that now bind her. In the beginning of the war the people of that section were told by Yankees that wished to raise regiments of soldiers to fight us, *that the Mississippi would be blocked against them*, when the very first act of the Confederate Congress insured the free navigation of the Mississippi river.

The Yankees say that by the first of July their public debt will be 650 million dollars! It is now 1,500 millions!! They have 65,000 sick from their own account. Who will pay their pensions?

This is a struggle on the side of the Yankees for supremacy, and on our side for independence. It is urged that the Northern States are a great deal stronger than the Southern States, and therefore must win in this contest. England was a great deal stronger than Scotland, but when it was the object of England to establish by force a supremacy over Scotland, they found the Scotch very ugly customers. In this war the North has had certain successes in the field. But how was it with England in the revolutionary war? It was not for want of victories in the field that England did not conquer the American colonies, for England found when most successful in the field, the object desired was as distant as before. It is not the question when endeavoring to conquer a country, whether you can break up its embattled armies and drive them off the plain, where they have contended with you in the fight. The question is this, and this alone, whether that country is set upon separation. If it is bent upon separation, it is impossible to conquer it, and if the North could conquer us. the political and civil difficulties remaining would render that success a curse and a misery to those who achieved it. It seems but homage to an abstract principle that has caused England to bear the misery consequent upon not recognising the Confederate States. There has been a sense of the danger and mischief of interference in intestine quarrels in other countries, and England has so far paid deference to that principle of international policy, but it will not last a great while longer.

The Yankees admit a loss of 10,000 men at Fort Donaldson—more I believe than we had engaged in the fight.

Sunday, June 15th. My cousin, S. M., called to see me to-day; also, my friends J. C. H. and F. N. B. I was allowed fifteen minutes conversation with each in the presence of a Federal commissioned officer, such being the rule established here. A sermon was preached to the prisoners to-day by the Rev. Mr. Nourse, from Leesburg, Virginia, himself a prisoner. William J Mills, Company D, 12th Georgia regiment, died to-day, and was buried at the " Congressional burying ground" in presence of a Confederate commissioned officer, taken there "for the purpose of witnessing" the same. A lady friend sent me a bottle of wine by the "Underground railroad." I cannot say with Hawthorne, to drink it is more a moral than a physical enjoyment, and that like whatever else which is superlatively good, it is better appreciated by memory than by present consciousness. It is decidedly physical in its effects, and far better in reality than in anticipation.

Monday, June 16th. Captain L. F Whitney, United States cavalry, called to see me to-day. Captain W. and myself were associated in the "draughtsman's room," United States Patent office, for nearly four years—every day engaged in the same calling, and upon terms of intimate friendship. One of his men now stands as sentinel to the room in which I am confined. Strange the mutations of time! Two years ago we would have laughed at the prophecy that we would at this time be in our present relations to each other. We talked only of the pleasures of the past without any allusion to our present difficulties, and the interview was, under the circumstances, short but agreeable. An old man was brought into our room to-day, and the officer who ushered him, remarked, as he did so, "Here is a man that wishes to see a live rebel." Lieutenant D. replied by informing him that "the man with horns" was out, but would soon be in. I presume the old fool became satisfied that we are beings of flesh and blood, who eat, drink, sleep, and wear clothes like other civilized people.

A fellow prisoner from Charlestown, Virginia, says when General Banks was at that place he stopped at a lady's boarding house without giving her any compensation. He sent the lady a few delicacies to eat while in her house, but when he went away he presented her a bill of $5.

Tuesday, June 17th. The Yankee newspapers claim a victory at Williamsburg. If that battle is a Federal triumph, they are welcome to all such. The fact is, that they have so much at stake, that they cannot afford to report their defeat, and do not scruple to lie! I feel very lonesome in this close room to-day, for those who share my captivity are reading, writing or sleeping, and I cannot do much of either, not more than record in my diary my present feelings. Solitude has the advantage or the danger of making us search more deeply into the same ideas. As our discourse is only with ourself, we always give the same direction to the conversation ; we are not called to turn it to the subject which occupies another mind, and so an involuntary inclination makes us return forever to knock at the same doors. There are eight officers in this room, and we take turns in put-

ting it in order, that is, folding up the blankets, sweeping out the room, &c., &c., and some take great interest in keeping the room clean, which is commendable. I distrust the intellect and morality of those people to whom disorder is of no consequence— who can live at ease in an Augean stable. What surrounds us, reflects more or less what is within us.

Wednesday, June 18th. A fellow prisoner, Mr. B., the able correspondent of the "London Times," handed me the following interesting article to read from the "London Morning Herald" of April 25th. The Herald is the organ of Earl Derby:

"The Southern Confederacy has nearly completed its sixteenth month of existence. In common parlance, in universal conviction, in actual fact, in everything but formal diplomatic recognition, the Confederate States are an independent power. The armies that have so long ravaged their frontiers, and at last emboldened by a great superiority of numbers, and a still greater advantage in arms and material, have ventured on an advance into their territory—*come there not as partizans in a civil war, but as invaders ;* they are and act as the enemies not of a faction but of a nation—nay, of the entire population. They find little sympathy, far less than was enjoyed by the French invaders of Spain. They obtain no information except that very scanty supply which the most hated enemy can always obtain from deserters ; they get no provisions except what they take by force ; they have no friends, and no power beyond their own lines. In saying this, we except, of course, that strip of mountains in Kentucky, Tennessee and Western Virginia, occupied by Northern colonists, and which is part of the Confederate States, simply by geographical position. It is very rare, as is evident to the most ignorant and violent of Northerners, to find a man that is within the Confederate lines who is not a devoted adherent of the Confederate Government, and a resolute defender of a country invaded by foreign armies. The Confederate Government has raised in proportion to its population as large an army as any country ever yet mustered ; it could have a still larger force if it had arms to put into their hands. It has sustained several great battles, won several brilliant victories, and rallied without difficulty or discouragement after one or two severe defeats. There is no division among the people ; no Unionist faction , there is no voice raised in favor of surrender. As the United States and the Confederate States form two separate and hostile nations, so the Confederate Government is clearly as independent of that of the Union as the Crown of Denmark of the Germanic Confederation, and is as completely organized and absolute within its own dominions as that which

is waging war against it. It is no question now of " Secession"
or Rebellion, but of a war between two distinct powers, *unequal
in numbers*, but perfectly equal in *strength and status*, equally
sovereign and equally national.   One may wrest territory from the
other, may plunder its lands, burn its towns, and blockade its
ports by virtue of superior naval and military force ; but the relation in which they stand to each other is not rebel and tyrant, not
subject and sovereign, but that of wholly separate and independent belligerent nations.   The Northern armies in Virginia or Tennessee are as the French in Spain, or Russia in Turkey—the sol-
diery of a foreign government engaged in the invasion of a soil to
which they have no other claim than may be established by the
strong hand, or bestowed by the fortunes of war.   The conquest
of one nation by another, rarely as it has occurred, is not wholly
unknown or impossible.   Poland is a conquered country, but for
western intervention Turkey might have been.   But the conquest
of a country as large as half of Europe, which brings three or four
hundred thousand of her sons to her defence, which is *fortified*
by *primeval forests* and *impenetrable swamps*, and impregnable
by sheer extent of uninhabitable surface, is one of the wildest
schemes ever proposed by the wickedness of demagogues, or en-
tertained by the madness of conceit.   A Napoleon with a half million of soldiers would recoil from the task.   Is a Lincoln with a
half a million of disorderly ruffians to achieve it?   The subjuga-
tion of the South is impossible, provided only the citizens of the
Confederate States display in defence of their hearths and homes,
of their rights and their country, the valor and the resolution
which have always characterized the race from which they sprang.
They are a superior race, and the children of cavaliers, and can
never yield to such an enemy   They have shown as yet no signs
of wavering or discouragement, and they have only to be resolute
in endurance, as they have shown themselves courageous in action, to be sure of a final victory   We see in the surrender of
Island No. 10, in the doubtful operations in Virginia, in the battle
near Pittsburgh, no signs whatever of any approach to the termination of the war in that way in which the North proposes to ter-
minate it, viz : by the total prostration of the Southern States, the
dissolution of the Confederacy, and the reconstruction of the
Union.   The Northern Government must be aware of the futility
of its promises, the utter impracticability of its professed designs ;
but the ignorant and fanatical North believe absolutely and pas-
sionately in their own omnipotence, and its rulers are not the men
to undertake the unpopular, difficult and dangerous task of bring-
ing the people to a more modest frame of mind.   Nothing but a
severe lesson, either a crushing defeat, or a long, expensive, result-
less and disastrous war will enlighten a people whose virtues or
weakness alike make them obstinate and unreasonable in such a

contest as the present. If left to themselves, *i. e.*, without foreign intervention, they will probably prolong the war into another year. One thing at least appears certain, that the summer must stay for some months, even under the most favorable circumstances, the onward march of the Federal armies. If they are able then to hold their actual positions—if they retain possession of the greater part of Tennessee, Kentucky, and Northern and Western Virginia—they will remain encamped on Southern soil, wasting the crops, burning the houses, taking property of the unhappy citizens of those rich States, but making no progress whatever. Their vessels may continue to keep up a nominal blockade of the Southern coast, and a real embargo on the cotton supply, which affords bread to South Lancastershire, England. In the meantime the Confederates will be daily gaining strength, recruiting their forces, and receiving supplies of arms and ammunition, the want of which has done more to thwart their heroic efforts than either the valor or bravery of Northern troops or skill of Northern commanders. On the return of cold weather their position will be better, and the termination of the war still more remote. In the interval they cannot invade the South, and cannot hope to hang the Confederate leaders, but they will still be starving English operatives, unless England and France grow weary of seeing their subjects made the victims of the war, and insist on terminating a struggle, which, while it cannot lead to the result desired by the aggressors, inflicts on neutrals losses almost as great as the immediate objects of the aggression."

A fellow prisoner showed me a beautiful love-letter he received from his affianced this morning by the "Underground railroad." The object of his affections is not permitted to visit him, because she has been herself a prisoner on account of her "Secession" convictions, but she brings a letter from Alexandria nearly every day, and sends to the "handsome Lieutenant :"

The letter! aye, the letter!
" 'Tis there a woman loves to speak her wishes ;
It spares the blushes of the love-sick maiden,
And every word's a smile, each line a tongue."

Thursday, June 19th. The only event of interest to me to-day has been the visit of an attached lady friend, Miss E. A., who brought me some necessary articles of clothing, quite acceptable under the circumstances, but more appreciated on account of the motive which prompted the mission. This lady has two brothers in the 17th regiment of Virginia volunteers. As an old friend, our interview of fifteen minutes afforded me

3

much pleasure ; but the Yankee officer present seemed desirous
to institute an espionage, more to annoy than to discharge his
orders, and which caused me to wish him in a climate where we
are told that the heat is intolerable—at all events during my
short interview with this to me beautiful angel of mercy. In
this despotic government I have noticed the ladies as well as the
sterner sex fear to express a sentiment against the tyranny of
him whom they call a Republican President. On the contrary
all must praise Abraham Lincoln, or be considered a traitor !
Great God, it seems as if they wish to honor themselves through
their master ; they elevate him on their shoulders as a pedestal ;
they surround him with a halo of light, in order that some of it
may be reflected on themselves. It is still the fable of the dog,
who contents himself with the chain and collar, so that they are
of gold.

June 20th. I received some excellent smoking tobacco and
cigars this morning, a present from a lady in Prince George
county, Maryland. God bless the ladies !

The "New York Times" of yesterday contains the following
in reference to my friend Captain Monaghan, of the sixth Louisiana regiment, who was paroled in the city during the first three
or four days after he arrived here :

(COPY OF PARAGRAPH.)

"THE LOUISIANA TIGER."

"Captain Manahan, of the Louisiana Tigers, who has been
lionizing at Willard's hotel for several days, has been sent to the
old capitol prison by order of Secretary Stanton. A gentleman,
formerly of New Orleans, and well acquainted with the Captain,
states that he does not wish to be exchanged, and is loyal to the
"Stars and Stripes."

The Captain being anxious to correct a statement so devoid of
truth, and which impeached his loyalty to the South, wrote to
the editor of the "New York Times," but as the sequel shows
he was not permitted to send the letter, and thus the ignorant
of the North were led to believe this lie, as they have thousands
of others circulated in the same way, and without the shadow of
foundation in truth :

"OLD CAPITOL PRISON, WASHINGTON, D. C., JUNE 20, 1862.

To the Editor of the New York Times,

SIR: A paragraph appeared in your edition of yesterday, headed " the Louisiana Tiger," and I infer that the informer, who furnished matter for this paragraph,

must have been made the dupe of a joker. I am no tiger, but the Captain of Company F, sixth regiment Louisiana volunteers. I have been on parole some days, anxiously awaiting an exchange. "Lionizing" is no amusement to me, but a great bore. My convictions, as well as my heart, are with my brethren, who are fighting in defence of my invaded country. I would that my strong right arm were there also. I trust this will be a sufficient answer to the New Orleans gentleman, who has *dared* to cast a stigma upon my loyalty and *devotion* to the *South;* and if further proof of the fact were necessary, it may be discovered in the act of Mr. Secretary Stanton, who has ordered me to be incarcerated in this place.

Respectfully your obedient servant,

WM. MONAGHAN,

Captain Company F, 6th Regiment Louisiana Volunteers,
Prisoner of War."

This letter was sent to the Provost Marshal for approval, but was returned with the following note from Mr. William P. Wood, the superintendent of the prison :

" OLD CAPITOL PRISON, JUNE 25, 1862.

The foregoing communication was placed in my hands by Captain Monaghan, to be examined at the Provost Marshal's office, and has been returned to me marked " not approved," and is returned to Captain M. by me, such being the usual procedure with letters " not approved."

WM. P. WOOD,
Superintendent."

Saturday, June 21st. P C. H. called to see me to-day. He is a clerk in the Adjutant General's office, but was formerly with me in the United States Patent office. A member of Company F, 35th Georgia, died in prison to-day, but I could not learn his name.

June 22d. The Rev. Father Boyle, (Catholic Priest,) called to see me to-day. He was allowed to come into my room alone, upon a promise not to talk about war matters. He brought me a copy of the " National Intelligencer" of June 12th, from which I extract the following :

" COTTON BURNING."

The London Star of May 27th thus appreciates the Confederate policy of cotton burning :

" If it be true that thousands of bales of goods—incapable of being converted into munitions of war, and absolutely secure, as private property, from confiscation by the Federals—are being burnt or rolled into the river, the Confederates are committing social as well as political suicide. It is an act that has no comparison in modern history. It is not, like the destruction of Moscow, an act of desperate patriotism, for it impoverishes the vanquished, without in the least injuring the victors. If all the cotton, tobacco and sugar between Richmond and Mobile were given to the flames, it would not retard by an hour the fall of those cities, nor enhance by a dollar the cost of the conquest. Neither can it be supposed, except by men whose offences and disasters have phrenzied their intellects, that these huge incendiarisms will attract the slightest favor to their cause from across the Atlantic. They must be mad, indeed, to reckon that England and France will come to the help of men who are wantonly injuring themselves and the subjects of those powers. The only kindness that Europe can show them, is to advise that they abstain from such barbarous outrages, and make their peace as quickly as they can with the government that is as superior in right as in strength, having both the right and the power to retaliate upon such atrocities by a splendid act of mercy to mankind."

ANOTHER BATTLE WITH JACKSON'S ARMY.

Advices received at the War Department state that Jackson's army attacked General Shields's advance on Monday morning, near Port Republic. The conflict is said to have been maintained for about four hours by about two thousand of our men against the main body of Jackson's army. The enemy's force became so overwhelming in number that our advance was compelled to fall back, which it did in good order, until it met the main body of General Shields's command, near Conrad's store. As soon as this was effected, the enemy in turn retired. The fighting is said to have been very severe, and the loss heavy on both sides. No further particulars have reached the department.

AN ACCOUNT OF THE BATTLE.

LURAY, VA., JUNE 10, 1862.

Colonel Carroll, commanding the fourth brigade, consisting of the eighty-fourth Pennsylvania, the eleventh Pennsylvania, the seventh Indiana, and the first Virginia regiments, altogether about sixteen hundred strong, reached Port Republic on Sunday, and reconnoitered and found the enemy in the town. They had a skirmish, and concluded to hold the bridge. They ordered it not to be burned, and put guns in position commanding it.

At six o'clock on Monday this battery was opened upon by some twenty heavy guns, which were placed in position during the night. Our forces tried to reach the bridge repeatedly to destroy it, but were met by storms of bullets, and had to retire. A large cavalry force crossed and attacked our troops, while their infantry followed our men, opposing them at every step, after driving them back with heavy loss; but our numbers, after General Tyler's third brigade arrived, were so much inferior to the enemy—theirs being at least five to one—that our position became so untenable, that it was impossible to hold it. We were therefore compelled to fall back, our boys fighting every foot of the way. After falling back some three or four miles, a body of cavalry were sent to attack us, but were received in such a manner as to compel them to retire, after which the engagement ended, having lasted about five hours.

Our loss in killed and wounded is not known, but it is large, as is also that of the enemy. We lost a large number of prisoners.

Colonel Carroll's horse fell, injuring the Colonel badly, and Captain Kelly, of General Shields's staff, was also much injured in the head. He received praise from all who witnessed his conduct in the action.

Colonel Buckley, of the 29th Ohio, was badly wounded. His men charged three times to obtain possession of his body, but it was carried off by the enemy.

General Ashby, of cavalry notoriety, was positively killed during the fight at the bridge over Middle river. Captain Keogh charged with a body of cavalry, and held the bridge some time during a terrible storm of grape.

This was one of the most hotly contested engagements of the whole war, as is indicated by the loss compared with the numbers engaged, who fought like demons.

Two regiments from the first brigade arrived in time to assist in covering the retreat. The pioneer corps also assisted. Colonel Buckley has arrived here wounded.

THE RETREAT OF GENERAL BANKS—HIS OFFICIAL REPORT.

Report of the march of the first division fifth corps d'armie from Strasburg, Virginia, to Williamsport, Maryland, on the 24th and 25th days of May, 1862.

HEADQUARTERS ARMY SHENANDOAH.

Hon. E. M. STANTON, *Secretary of War.*

Information was received on the evening of May 23d, that the enemy, in very large force, had descended on the guard at Front Royal, Colonel Kenly, first Maryland regiment, commanding, burning the bridges and driving our troops toward Strasburg with great loss. Owing to what was deemed an extravagant statement of the enemy's strength, these reports were received with some distrust; but a regiment of infantry, with a strong detachment of cavalry and a section of artillery, were immediately sent to reinforce Colonel Kenly. Later in the evening despatches from fugitives who had escaped to Winchester informed us that Colonel Kenly's force had been destroyed, with but few exceptions, and the enemy, 15,000 or 20,000 strong, were advancing by rapid marches on Winchester.

Orders were immediately given to halt the reinforcements sent to Front Royal, which had moved by different routes, and detachments of troops, under experienced officers, were sent in every direction to explore the roads leading from Front Royal to Strasburg, Middletown, Newtown and Winchester, to ascertain the force, position and purpose of this sudden movement of the enemy. It was soon found that his pickets were in possession of every road, and rumors from every quarter represented him in movement, in the rear of his pickets, in the direction of our camp.

The extraordinary force of the enemy could no longer be doubted. It was apparent, also, that they had a more extended purpose than the capture of the brave little band at Front Royal.

This purpose could be nothing less than the defeat of my own command, or its possible capture by occupying Winchester, and by this movement intercepting supplies or reinforcements, and cutting off all possibility of retreat.

It was also apparent, from the reports of fugitives, prisoners, Union men, and our own reconnoitering parties, that the three divisions of the enemy's troops, known to be in the valley, and embracing at least 25,000 men, were united and close upon us, in some enterprise not yet developed.

The suggestion, that had their object been a surprise, they would not have given notice of their approach by an attack on Front Royal, was answered by the fact, that on the only remaining point of attack—the Staunton road—our outposts were five miles in advance, and daily reconnoissances made for a distance of twelve miles towards Woodstock.

Under this interposition of the enemy's plans, our position demanded instant decision and action. Three courses were open to us : First, a retreat across Little North Mountain to the Potomac river, on the west. Second, an attack upon the enemy's flank on the Front Royal road. Third, a rapid movement direct upon Winchester, with a view to anticipate his occupation of the town by seizing it ourselves, thus placing my command in communication with its original base of operations, in the line of reinforcements by Harper's Ferry and Martinsburg, and securing a safe retreat in case of disaster.

To remain at Strasburg was to be surrounded ; to move over the mountains was to abandon our train at the outset, and to subject my command to flank attacks, without possibility of succor ; and to attack the enemy in such overwhelming force could only result in certain destruction. It was, therefore, determined to enter the lists with the enemy in a race or a battle, as he should choose, for the possession of Winchester, the key of the valley, and for us the position of safety.

THE MARCH.

At three o'clock, A. M., the 24th instant, the reinforcements, infantry, artillery and cavalry, sent to Colonel Kenly, were recalled ; the advance guard, Colonel

Donnelly's brigade, were ordered to return to Strasburg. Several hundred disabled men, left in our charge by Shields' division, were put upon the march, and our wagon train ordered forward to Winchester under escort of cavalry and infantry. General Hatch, with nearly our whole force of cavalry, and six pieces of artillery, was charged with the protection of the rear of the column, and the destruction of army stores, for which transportation was not provided, with instructions to remain in front of the town as long as possible, and hold the enemy in check, our expectations of attack being in that direction. All these orders were executed with incredible alacrity, and soon after nine o'clock the column was on the march, Colonel Donnelly in front, Colonel Gordon in the centre, and General Hatch in the rear.

The column had passed Cedar creek, about three miles from Strasburg, with the exception of the rear guard, still in front of Strasburg, when information was received from the front that the enemy had attacked the train, and was in full possession of the road at Middletown. This report was confirmed by the return of fugitives, refugees and wagons, which came tumbling to the rear in fearful confusion.

It being apparent now that our immediate danger was in front, the troops were ordered to the head of the column, and the train to the rear, and, in view of a possible necessity of our return to Strasburg, Captain James W. Albert, Topographical corps, who associated with him the Zouaves D'Afrique, Captain Collis, was ordered to prepare Cedar creek bridge for the flames, in order to prevent a pursuit in that direction by the enemy. In the execution of this order Captain Albert and the Zouaves were cut off from the column, which they joined at Williamsport. They had at Strasburg a sharp conflict with the enemy, in which his cavalry suffered severely. An interesting report of this affair will be found in the reports of Captain Albert and Captain Collis.

THE FIRST CONFLICT.

The head of the reorganized column, Colonel Donnelly commanding, encountered the enemy in force at Middletown, about thirteen miles from Winchester. Three hundred troops had been seen in town, but it soon appeared that larger forces were in the rear. The brigade halted, and the forty-sixth Pennsylvania, Colonel Knipe, was ordered to penetrate the woods on the right and dislodge the enemy's skirmishers. They were supported by a section of Cochran's New York battery. Five companies of the enemy's cavalry were discovered in an open field in the rear of the woods, and our artillery, masked at first by the infantry, opened fire upon them. They stood fire for a while, but at length retreated, pursued by our skirmishers. The twenty eighth New York, Lieutenant Colonel Brown, was now brought up, and under a heavy fire of infantry and artillery the enemy were driven back more than two miles from the pike. Colonel Donnelly being informed at that point by a citizen, in great alarm, that four thousand men were in the woods beyond, the men were anxious to continue the fight; but as this would have defeated our object by the loss of valuable time, with the exception of a small guard, they were ordered to resume the march.

This affair occurred under my own observation, and I have great pleasure in vouching for the admirable conduct of officers and men. We lost one man killed and some wounded. The loss of the enemy could not be ascertained.

This episode, with the change of front, occupied nearly an hour, but it saved our column. Had the enemy vigorously attacked our train while at the head of the column, it would have been thrown into such dire confusion as to have made a successful continuation of our march impossible. Pending this contest, Colonel Broadhead, of the first Michigan cavalry, was ordered to advance, and, if possible, to cut his way through and occupy Winchester. It was the report of this energetic officer that gave us the first assurance that our course was yet clear, and he was the first of our column to enter the town.

THE SECOND COMBAT.

When it was first reported that the enemy had pushed between us and Winchester, General Hatch was ordered to advance with all his available cavalry from Strasburg, leaving Colonel De Forrest to cover the rear, and destroy stores not provided with transportation. Major Vought, fifth New York cavalry, had been previously ordered to reconnoitre the Front Royal road to ascertain the position of the enemy, whom he encountered in force near Middletown, and was compelled to fall back, immediately followed by the enemy's cavalry, infantry and artillery. In this affair five of our men were killed and several wounded. The enemy's loss is not known.

After repeated attempts to force a passage through the lines of the enemy, now advanced to the pike, General Hatch, satisfied that this result could not be accomplished without great loss, and supposing our army to have proceeded but a short distance, turned to the left, and moving upon a parallel road, made several ineffectual attempts to effect a junction with the main column. At Newtown, however, he found Colonel Gordon holding the enemy in check, and joined his brigade. Major Collins, with three companies of cavalry, mistaking the point where the main body of the cavalry left the road, dashed upon the enemy until stopped by a barricade of wagons, and the tempestuous fire of infantry and artillery. His loss must have been severe.

Six companies of the fifth New York, Colonel De Forrest, and six companies of the first Vermont cavalry, Colonel Tompkins, after repeated and desperate efforts to effect a junction with the main body—the road now being filled with infantry, artillery and cavalry—fell back to Strasburg, where they found the Zouaves D' Afrique. The fifth New York, failing to effect a junction at Winchester, and also at Martinsburg, came in at Clear Spring, with a train of thirty two wagons and many stragglers. The first Vermont, Colonel Tompkins, joined us at Winchester, with six pieces of artillery, and participated in the fight of the next morning. Nothing could surpass the celerity and spirit with which the various companies of cavalry executed their movements, or their intrepid charges upon the enemy.

General Hatch deserves great credit for the manner in which he discharged his duties as chief of cavalry in this part of our march, as well as at the fight at Winchester, and in covering the rear of our column to the river; but especially for the spirit infused into his troops during the brief period of his command, which, by confession of friend and foe, had been equal if not superior to the best of the enemy's long trained mounted troops.

From this point the protection of the rear of the column devolved upon the forces under Colonel Gordon.

THE THIRD COMBAT.

The-guard having been separated from the column, and the rear of the train having been attacked by an increased force near the bridge between Newtown and Kearnstown, Colonel Gordon was directed to send back the second Massachusetts, Lieutenant Colonel Brown to rescue the rear of the train and hold the enemy in check. They found him at Newtown, with a strong force of infantry, cavalry and artillery.

The second Massachusetts was employed in the field, supported by the twenty-eighth New York and twenty-seventh Indiana, and ordered to drive the enemy from the town, and the battery was at the same time so placed as to silence the guns of the enemy.

Both these objects were quickly accomplished. They found it impossible to reach Middletown, so as to enable the cavalry under General Hatch to join the column, or to cover entirely the rear of the train. Large bodies of the enemy's cavalry passed upon our right and left, and the increased vigor of his movements demonstrated the rapid advance of the main body. A cavalry charge made upon our troops was received in squares on the right and on the road, and in the line of the left, which repelled his assault, and gained time to reform the train, to cover its rear, and to burn the disabled wagons. This affair occupied several hours—the regiments having been moved to the rear about six o'clock, and not reaching the town until after twelve.

A full report by Colonel Gordon, who commanded in person, is enclosed herewith. The principal loss of the second Massachusetts occurred in this action.

THE FIGHT AT WINCHESTER.

The strength and purpose of the enemy were to us unknown when we reached Winchester, except upon surmise and vague rumors from Front Royal. These rumors were strengthened by the vigor with which the enemy had pressed our main column, and defeated at every point efforts of detachments to effect a junction with the main column.

At Winchester, however, all suspicion was relieved on that subject, all classes—Secessionists, Unionists, Refugees and Prisoners—agreed that the enemy's force at or near Winchester was overwhelming, ranging from 25,000 to 30,000. Rebel officers, who came into our camp with entire unconcern, supposing that their own troops occupied the town, as a matter of course, and were captured, confirmed these statements, and added that an attack would be made on us at daybreak. I determined to test the substance and strength of the enemy by actual collision, and measures were promptly taken to prepare our troops to meet them. They had taken up their positions on entering the town after dark, without expectation of a battle, and were at disadvantage, as compared with the enemy.

The rolling of musketry was heard during the latter part of the night, and before the break of day a sharp engagement occurred at the outposts. Soon after four o'clock the artillery opened its fire, which continued without cessation till the close of the engagement.

The right of our line was occupied by the third brigade, Colonel George H. Gordon commanding. The regiments were strongly posted, and near the centre covered by stone walls from the fire of the enemy.

Their infantry opened on the right, and soon both lines were under heavy fire.

The left was occupied by the third brigade, Colonel Dudley Donnelly commanding.

The line was weak, compared with that of the enemy, but the troops were posted, and patiently awaited, as they nobly improved their coming opportunity. The earliest movements of the enemy were on our left, two regiments being sent to move, as with the purpose of occupying a position in flank or rear. General Hatch sent a detachment of cavalry to intercept this movement, when it was apparently abandoned. The enemy suffered very serious loss from the fire of our infantry on the left. One regiment is represented by persons present during the action and after the field was evacuated as nearly destroyed.

The main body of the enemy was hidden during the early part of the action by the crest of the hill and the woods in the rear.

Their force was massed apparently upon our right, and their manœuvres indicated a purpose to turn us upon the Berryville road, where it appeared subsequently they had placed a considerable force, with a view of preventing reinforcements from Harper's Ferry. But the steady fire of our lines held them in check, until a small portion of the troops, on the right of our line, made a movement to the rear. It is but just to add that this was done under the erroneous impression that an order to withdraw had been given. No sooner was this observed by the enemy, than its regiments swarmed upon the crest of the hill, advancing from the woods upon our right, which, still continuing its fire steadily, withdrew towards the town.

The overwhelming force of the enemy, now suddenly showing itself, making further resistance unwise, orders were sent to the left by Captain De Hauteville to withdraw, which was done reluctantly, but in order, the enemy having greatly suffered in the wing. A portion of the troops passed through the town in some confusion, but the column was soon reformed, and continued its march in order. This engagement held the enemy in check five hours.

The forces engaged were greatly unequal. Indisposed to accept the early rumors concerning the enemy's strength, I reported to the department that it was about 15,000. It is now conclusively shown that not less than 25,000 men were in position, and could have been brought into action. On the right and left their great superiority of numbers was plainly felt and seen, and the signal officers, from elevated positions, were enabled to count regimental standards, indicating a strength equal to that above stated.

My own command consisted of two brigades of less than four thousand men, all told, with nine hundred cavalry, ten Parrott guns, and one battery of six-pounders, smooth bore cannon. To this should be added the tenth Maine regiment of infantry, and five companies of Maryland cavalry, stationed at Winchester, which were engaged in the action. The loss of the enemy was treble that of ours in killed and wounded. In prisoners ours greatly exceeded theirs.

Officers, whose word I cannot doubt, have stated, as the result of their own observation, that our men were fired upon from private dwellings in passing through Winchester; but I am credibly informed, and gladly believe, that the atrocities said to have been perpetrated upon our wounded soldiers by the rebels are greatly exaggerated, or entirely untrue.

Our march was turned in the direction of Martinsburg, hoping there to meet with reinforcements—the troops moving in three parallel columns, each protected by an efficient rear guard. Pursuit by the enemy was prompt and vigorous, but our movements were rapid, and without loss.

A few miles from Winchester the sound of a steam whistle, heard in the direction of Martinsburg, strengthened the hope of reinforcements, and stirred the blood of the men like a trumpet. Soon after two squadrons of cavalry came dashing down the road with wild hurrahs. They were thought to be the advance of the anticipated support, and were received with deafening cheers. Every man felt like turning back upon the enemy. It proved to be the first Maryland cavalry, Lieutenant Colonel Metschky, sent out in the morning as a train guard. Hearing the guns, they had returned to participate in the fight.

Advantage was taken of this stirring incident to reorganize our column, and the march was continued with renewed spirit and order. At Martinsburg the column halted two and a half hours, the rear guard remaining until seven in the evening in rear of the town, and arrived at the river at sundown, forty-eight hours after the first news of the attack on Front Royal. It was a march of fifty-three miles, thirty-five of which were performed in one day. The scene at the river when the rear guard arrived was of the most animating and exciting description. A thousand camp fires were burning on the hill side; a thousand carriages of every description were crowded upon the banks of the broad river between the exhausted troops and their coveted rest.

The ford was too deep for the teams to cross in regular succession; only the strongest horses, after a few experiments, were allowed to essay the passage of the river before morning. The single ferry was occupied by the ammunition trains, the ford by the wagons. The cavalry was secure in its form of crossing. The troops only had no transportation. Fortunately the train we had so sedulously guarded served us in turn. Several boats belonging to the pontoon train, which we had brought from Strasburg, were launched, and devoted exclusively to their service. It is seldom that a river crossing of such magnitude is achieved with greater success. There never were more grateful hearts in the same number of men then when at midday on the 20th we stood on the opposite shore.

My command had not suffered an attack and rout, but accomplished a premeditated march of nearly sixty miles in the face of the enemy, defeating his plans and giving him battle wherever he was found.

Our loss is stated in detail, with the names of the killed, wounded and missing, in the full report of Brigadier General A. S. Williams, commanding division, to which reference is made. The whole number in killed is 38, wounded 155, missing 711. Total loss 905.

It is undoubtedly true that many of the missing will yet return, and the entire loss may be assumed as not exceeding seven hundred. It is also probable that the number of killed and wounded may be larger than that above stated, but the aggregate loss will not be changed thereby. All our guns were saved.

Our wagon train consisted of nearly five hundred wagons. Of this number fifty-five were lost. They were not, with a few exceptions, abandoned to the enemy, but were burned upon the road. Nearly all of our supplies were thus saved. The stores at Front Royal, of which I had no knowledge until my visit to that position on the 21st instant, and those at Winchester, of which a considerable portion was destroyed by our troops, are not embraced in this statement.

4

The number of sick men in the hospital at Strasburg, belonging to General Williams's division was 189, 125 of whom were left in the hospital at Winchester, under charge of surgeon Lincoln R. Stone, second Massachusetts, or were left in hospital at Strasburg, including attendants, under charge of surgeon Gillespie, seventh Indiana, and assistant surgeon Porter, United States army.

Eight of the surgeons of this division voluntarily surrendered themselves to the enemy, in the hospitals and on the field, for the care of the sick and wounded placed under their charge. They include, in addition to those above named, brigade surgeon Peale, at Winchester; surgeon Mitchell, first Maryland, at Front Royal; surgeon Adolphus, Bests's battery, United States army; surgeon Johnson, sixteenth Indiana; and surgeon Francis Leland, second Massachusetts, on the field.

It is seldom that men are called upon to make a greater sacrifice of comfort, health and liberty, for the benefit of those entrusted to their charge. Services and sacrifices like these ought to entitle them to some more important recognition of their devotion to public duty than the mere historical record of the fact.

The report of the medical director, surgeon W. S. King, exhibits the disposition of nearly one thousand sick and disabled men left at Strasburg by Shields's division upon its removal to the Rappahannock valley.

My warmest thanks are due to the officers and men of my command for their unflinching courage and unyielding spirit exhibited on the march and its attendant combats. Especially to Brigadier General A. S. Williams, commanding the division, General George S. Greene, and General L. W. Crawford, who had reported for duty, but were yet unassigned to separate commands They accompanied the column throughout the march, and rendered me most valuable assistance.

My thanks are also due to the gentlemen of my staff—Major D. D. Perkins, chief of staff; Captain James W Albert, of the Topographical Engineers ; Captain Wm. Sheffler, Captain Frederick Munther, and Captain Frederick De Hauteville—for their arduous labors.

It gives me pleasure also to commend the conduct of Colonel Donnelly and Colonel Gordon, commanding the two brigades. I would also respectfully ask the attention of the department to the reports of the several officers commanding detachments separate from the main column, and to the officers named in the report of General Williams, as worthy of commendation for meritorious conduct.

The signal corps, Lieutenant W W Rowley commanding, rendered most valuable service on the field and in the march. There should be some provision for the prompt promotion of officers and men so brave and useful as those composing this corps. The safety of the train and supplies is, in a great degree, due to the discretion, experience, and unfailing energy of Captain S. B. Holabird and Captain E. G. Beckwith, United States army.

I have the honor to be, with great respect,

Your obedient servant,

N. P. BANKS,
Major General Commanding.

June 24th, 1862. Subjoined is a letter from that Southern traitor and unscrupulous scoundrel, " Parson Brownlow," to the " Philadelphia Enquirer :"

Extracts from Northern papers.

EAST TENNESSEE.

Editor Philadelphia Inquirer :

Sir—I have two letters of recent date, and from reliable sources, giving me news from East Tennessee, which I desire to place you in possession of, and through you the public generally.

The persecutions of the Union men continue, and really increase in severity.

The property of all Union men in the Federal States and army was being sold at auction, including furniture, stock, grain, agricultural implements, &c., no attention being paid to the necessities of their families. The Union citizens and soldiers, who are in the prisons of Salisbury, Tuscaloosa and Mobile, are dying rapidly from the effects of tainted meat, rotten food, and starvation. The Rebel authorities seek to dispose of Union men in this way.

The whole country in East Tennessee is filled with guerrilla bands, who are committing all sorts of depredations on Union people, and destroying their property The Union men in the United States army, at Cumberland Gap, are breathing threatening and slaughter against the despoilers of their homes, the consumers of their substance, and the murderers of their parents and relatives, and nothing but the direct interference of Providence will prevent them from executing their threats. No military discipline will be sufficiently strong to prevent these men from the indiscriminate slaughter of those Secession leaders and soldiers who have done all this mischief.

One of the letters before me is from a Union officer at Cumberland Gap, and is dated June 27th. It gives this information: "Duncan McCall is just over from Knox county, and reports eight thousand Rebel troops at Knoxville, who were going to Atlanta, Georgia, by way of Maryville, distant only sixteen miles from Knoxville. The Secesh citizens had their goods packed up and marked for Atlanta, and were themselves crossing the river at Knoxville. The Rebels had arrested Montgomery Thornburg, Lemuel Johnson, Esquire Galbraith, Oliver P. Temple, John Baxter and others, and sent them to Tuscaloosa. Thornburg and Temple were dead, and the remains of the former had been brought back. Others were lying at the point of death."

Colonel Thornburg was the commonwealth's attorney, and visited my bedside the night before I was started out of the bogus Confederacy, upon a pass granted him by the commanding officer. When he took leave of me he held me by the hand, and with tears in his eyes, made this remark: "Brownlow, I am glad you are going out, and I hope you may arrive safe; but God only knows what will become of those of us who remain!"

Colonel Temple was a good lawyer, in comfortable circumstances, and as noble a man as lived in Tennessee. He was a Bell Everett elector for that district in the late election for President. He leaves a wife and one child to mourn his loss. He had been my friend through evil and good report.

Colonel Baxter is a wealthy lawyer, of fine talents, and a citizen of Knoxville. He has been my friend for years, and I sympathize with his wife and ten interesting children. Certainly nothing short of an old fashioned orthodox *hell* will suit as a place of confinement for the persecutors of these Union men.

July 9, 1862.   W. G. BROWNLOW.

Extracts from Northern papers.

THE CONFEDERATE GENERAL JACKSON.

General Jackson was educated at West Point, and was afterwards a professor for fifteen years at the Virginia Military School at Lexington. He is a cousin of the Jackson who was once Lieutenant Governor of Virginia, and of the Jackson who is now the United States District Judge for Western Virginia. The family settled early in that region, and furnished its representative in Congress for about thirty years, commencing with the administration of General Washington. It has become a numerous family in the Valley of Virginia and in Western Virginia, and its members are about equally divided by the present struggle. After his hard fight of last Sunday with General Fremont, in which he was compelled to leave the field, he attacked the next day and drove back an advanced force of two thousand men of the army of General Shields. Such persistency proves that he has the confidence of his troops, and he doubtless deserves it. He has been the fighting hero of the war on the Confederate side.—*Washington Republican.*

THE REVEALING OF THE GRAVES AT CORINTH.

Suspicions of the contents of some of the graves found in the vicinity of Corinth, caused an investigation and exhuming of the deposits. Neatly made graves, with necessary head and foot boards, bearing the names of colonels and majors were visited, and the loose earth covering them was ordered to be removed, when, on arriving to the depth of four feet, a solid substance was struck, which upon clearing the earth around, was found to be contraband Secesh, in the shape of siege guns. One grave with the head-board designated as "Colonel somebody," was found to contain a 64-pounder siege gun. "Quite a heavy colonel that." Others were found, but in what number I have not learned. Some have been found buried in the swamps beyond Corinth.— *Correspondent Cincinnati Times.*

THE BLACKEST PAGE.

When the truthful historian shall write the history of this sad and unholy civil war, there will be in the volume many pages over which a shadow of blackness will forever rest; but the blackest page will be that which hands down to future generations the record of General Butler's order in regard to the women of New Orleans. Like the shadow of a great wrong, it will forever darken the fair brow of the Goddess of Liberty. The millions yet unborn will read it with commingled feelings of shame and pity, and doubt our boasted claim to freedom, civilization and Christianity. True, it is but the act of one man, but that man commissioned and paid by his country for the enforcement of the laws and the preservation of society. If the government retains him in commission, it becomes responsible for his acts, and endorses his infamy.

No man respects more than we do the well-earned reputation of the American army:

> " It is a school
> Where every principle tending to honor
> Is taught—*if followed;*

but in the name of that distinguished army we solemnly protest against an act which would blight its greenest laurels, and lay its trophies prostrate in the dust. If they war, let it not be done on domestic happiness; if they invade, be their country's hearths inviolable; let them achieve a triumph wherever their banners fly, but be it not over morals, innocence and virtue.

Let the government remove this stigma from its name by removing General Butler from his command.—*Ohio Dayton Empire, June 7.*

There is a United States Court at Washington city which makes a business of catching and surrendering persons claimed as fugitive slaves, and refuses to hear evidence that the claimants are traitors. If anybody wants to be taxed for the support of such a court, let him be so taxed; we don't. How many judicial functionaries, beginning with Chief Justice Roger B. Taney, are taking pay from the United States, while their hearts are with the Southern Confederacy, we cannot say; but we think the number ought to be reduced. Who shall devise the proper mode ?—*New York Tribune.*

June 25th. To-day a lady from Alexandria, Virginia, called to see a prisoner, and the latter remarked to her that he had suffered very much since his confinement from sickness and privation, and the lady replied, "Well, you must bear it manfully, you are doing what you believe to be your duty," whereupon the Yankee Lieutenant present, whose name is Holmes, told her she "must leave the room, or she would be arrested." The Rev. Mr. Nourse, heretofore permitted to preach funeral sermons over prisoners who have died here, has been superseded on the charge of uttering Secession sentiments. Having heard every sermon he has preached, I can truthfully record that he has not at any time said anything which could be *tortured* into " Secession sentiments." They must have objected to the repetition by Mr. Nouise of the commandments : " Thou shalt not steal," or " thou shalt not covet thy neighbor's man servant, nor his maid servant," &c. ; for no doubt their guilty consciences caused them to feel pain upon the utterance of these imperative injunctions from Holy Writ, and some one of them were compelled to be present on such an occasion :

Extracts from Northern papers.

FROM THE SHENANDOAH—HOW MATTERS STAND IN THE VALLEY.

Correspondence of the Cincinnati Times.

WINCHESTER, June 18.—At the present writing, I think it is safe, in consideration of the time which must elapse before the publication of my letter, to state that, though I have industriously sought for information, I have yet to find the first officer of any military importance who has any hesitancy in stating that he considers their condition of the most critical character. What renders it the more so at present is the fact that the whereabouts of Jackson is not known. He may be moving on Front Royal to attack Shields, or he may be circumventing the Strasburg Mountain to get in the rear of Fremont. Every precaution is being used that human or military ingenuity can invent, in the way of scouts and videttes, but the troops are limited in number and worn out by their late duties, while the country is extensive and well suited for the purposes of war, to a people who know the windings of every mountain road, and whose spies are like the cattle of Ossian's hero "on a thousand hills."

Further than this, Secessia fights its battles in the valleys, in the midst of its friends. The farmer who refuses a particle of food to the Union traveler, although the latter is willing to pay for it, is ever ready to turn out all he has to the Confederate army—first, because he really sympathizes with the Confederate soldiers, and, secondly, because he fears to withhold what he is confident they will take whether he is willing or not.

MORE FORCES WANTED.

As I have said in almost every letter I have ever written you from this quarter, the general cry is "We want more troops in the Valley." An application, as I stated, has been made to Secretary Stanton, and I understand it is now to be backed by the urgent persuasions of two other members of the Cabinet, who are convinced of the insufficiency of the force in this section.

A small portion of the force here has been sent to Hagerstown, Williamsport and Martinsburg, to guard those points, and I think the movement is a very wise one. The 84th Ohio Regiment, one of the new Regiments, has arrived at Cumberland, and it will probably take the place of some of those more experienced, and act as post garrisons, while those heretofore engaged in that duty will be called to more active service.

Rumors are abroad as to the expected arrival of a portion of General Halleck's force in this quarter, but I can see no reliable foundation for the rumor.

FRONT ROYAL OR MOUNT JACKSON?

Public opinion, and by that I mean military speculation, is just now strongly divided as to whether that arch traitor, Jackson, is still in front of Mount Jackson, or is wending his way toward a meditated attack on General Shields, at Front Royal. I am somewhat inclined to think it is toward the latter. As I am now situated, I am an "intermediate circumstance" between the two points.

WHERE WILL JACKSON STRIKE?—TROUBLE AMONG THE FEDERAL TROOPS.

MIDDLETOWN, June 19.—Everything to-day bears the appearance of a "muss," to come off somewhere in this region almost immediately. Whether this will be on the Mount Jackson road, or at Front Royal, as I stated in my former letter, it is impossible for me yet to say, but I listen for the tidings hourly which shall announce the opening of the battle. Matters point most directly to Front Royal, yet with the acuteness of General Jackson to manage Secession affairs, it may break upon us from some of the mountain defiles either beyond that point or over on the Mount Jackson road, or just as likely in the immediate vicinity of this place, or, again, between here and Winchester, in our rear.

With the condition of feeling that I know to exist among both officers and men on the National side, I have no hesitation to state that after a hotly contested field, the result of the battle will be another grand "skedaddle." The knowledge that Jackson has been heavily reinforced is patent to every private in our ranks, and that consequence must ensue which attends as a certainty upon the efforts of men who fight under discouraging circumstances. The retreat of June 2d is still fresh in their minds, and the failure of the War Department to properly reinforce the division in the Mountain Department, I believe, will be productive of results greatly to be deplored. I may be mistaken in my conjectures, but I give you my impressions, and leave to time to prove their correctness or falsity. The electric wire may have notified you before this reaches you, relative to what I say. I repeat, something is on the eve of being accomplished, and only a change produced by unforeseen circumstances will prevent its accomplishment.

ARRIVAL OF CONFEDERATE PRISONERS AT PHILADELPHIA.

From the Philadelphia Inquirer, June 25.

Four hundred and ninety Confederate prisoners, taken recently at various points in the Shenandoah Valley, arrived from Harrisburg last evening, and at half past eight reached Washington street wharf, whence they left the cars for the steamboat Major Reybold, which transported them to Fort Delaware. Of these men four hundred and thirty-four arrived in Harrisburg on the 16th instant, and fifty-eight the day before yesterday, making in all four hundred and ninety-two, of whom two still remain sick in Harrisburg. They had among them but one officer, Major Davis, of the 2d Virginia Infantry, who had been at the battle of Bull Run, and in all the engagements since fought in the valley, under Jackson.

He is a native of Jefferson county, Virginia, is very prepossessing and gentlemanly, and about 35 years of age. His coat was of fine grey cloth, with abundant gold lace on the arms and collar; his pantaloons were of light army blue, and his cap of the same color. The prisoners were under charge of a guard, commanded by Lieutenant-Colonel Thompson, of the 115th Pennsylvania Regiment, and appeared in good spirits, taking their present and anticipated confinement with great philosophy. Many were from Northern States, and not a few from Massachusetts. Irishmen were by no means unfrequent among them.

The account given by Northern men and foreigners generally was, that they were pressed into the service, or enlisted through want of employment and the means of living. The whole gang were exceedingly sun-burnt and rugged through exposure and incessant marching, and in an inconceivably filthy state, their clothing being filled with vermin. The prisoners were in sixteen cars, of which nearly all were freight cars. Each of these, on arrival, was surrounded by crowds who entered into conversation with the prisoners. One Confederate was asked if he would take the oath of allegiance, and answered, "I'll see you —— first."

Another asked if it was true that McClellan was dead. "You'll hear about that when he gets into Richmond," said one of the crowd. "He'd better hurry up, then," was the reply. "You know he said he was going to be there on the 4th of July, he has only nine days ahead of him." In answer to the numerous charges of cruelty urged against the Confederates, both towards wounded men and towards prisoners, this was denied as regards the mass of the Confederate army, but it was allowed that individual cases might have been perpetrated by the "Pineys," or ignorant backwoodsmen of the South. The prisoners claimed that the Confederates were men, as were the Unionists, and would act towards their fellow-creatures fully as well.

THE REBEL ASHBY.

From our own Correspondent.

BALTIMORE, June 16, 1862.

Turner Ashby belonged to Fauquier county, where his family was influential, if not wealthy. In Washington, Baltimore and Richmond, the Ashbys were well known among people of superior social position, and were everywhere esteemed for their intelligence, courage and honor. But the refinement which seems to have been a characteristic of the same, must have met with an exception in the "Black-Horse" Colonel, who is always described as brusque, stern, soldier-like.

His earliest military experience, beyond the mere soldier-playing of Virginia horsemen, was in command of a company of cavalry, whom he led to Charlestown immediately upon the apparition of John Brown at Harper's Ferry. It was then and there that Ashby's "Black-Horse" had their name; his men were mounted on blooded black chargers, and the chargers were mounted by "blooded" white riders—horse and man alike were of the first families. His men were picked for their equestrian accomplishments, and many of their horses were bred and trained on his own plantation. As for himself, his name as a horseman is famous from Washington to Winchester, his repute in this respect being equal to that of the gallant, but reckless Randolph Ridgely, of Baltimore, to the exploits of whose battery in Mexico, Colonel May is mainly indebted for his dragoon reputation.

During the John Brown affair, Ashby scouted the Shenandoah county for negro conspirators, and effectually checked the spirit of servile uprising. He was one of the first to enlist in the Rebellion, and waited in Richmond with a proffer of his services, till the ordinance of Secession was passed. That same day, he hurried to Harper's Ferry, by way of Washington the "Relay," and followed by several Virginians, was the first mounted Rebel to rush into that storied little town. It is believed that the movement against Harper's Ferry was proposed and organized at Richmond by him.

Turner Ashby was a *gentle* man—so quiet, taciturn, and reticent, as to be thought morose by those who did not know him well. If a Rebel can be pious, he was so. I have heard from two intelligent residents of Harper's Ferry, that he especially abominated profanity, and when in that place, last fall, he was excited for a moment into *damning* something, he openly expressed his regret and mortification.

It was certain that he was not ambitious of military honors, for he was twice offered the shoulder-straps of a brigadier general, but declined, on the ground that he had no special military fitness, save for the command of cavalry, composed of men whom he knew, and in a region with which he was familiar. When, finally, he did accept the brigadier's commission, it was for expediency, and in compliance with urgent appeals.

His younger brother "Dick," a captain in his own corps, was peculiarly endeared to him by his fine horsemanship, and his personal intrepidity. Dick Ashby, you remember, was killed in a desperate affair with Wallace's Indiana Zouaves, near Patterson's Creek, on the Baltimore and Ohio Railroad. After his horse was killed, and he was shot, he refused quarter, and kicked at our men as he lay on the ground. It is said by all who knew him, that Turner Ashby has been a silent, but a savage, man ever since.

He was about thirty-seven years old, of medium height, weighing, perhaps, 150 pounds, of very dark complexion, with deeply set black eyes, surmounted by shaggy eye-brows, and with a most imposing beard and moustache, covering half of his face, and falling half way down his breast.

He was devoted to General Jackson, and frequently declared that he should be proud to follow him in any character, and for any duty. As for his personal courage, it is enough to say that the very morning General Banks entered Winchester, Ashby went to his headquarters disguised as a market man, and in reply to questions from staff officers, described his Rebel self.

The day before the battle of Winchester, he rode through the streets of that town, with one of his Captains, in Union uniform.

One of the most gallant Colonels in Shields's command, who has observed Ashby in three engagements, said in a verbal report to Government, a few days ago, that the Black-Horse General had of late become the most reckless man to be found on either side; that he seemed to plunge into all forms of danger with delight, riding wherever the fire was hottest, waving his sword, discharging his pistol at our best officers, and continually inviting hand-to-hand encounters. Our Colonel saw him leap his horse over an abandoned gun, to make such an attack. So peculiar, by its skill and daring, was his horsemanship, that he long ago became a marked man, and General Shields predicted that Ashby would surely be killed before Jackson was driven out of the valley. It was no doubt an intelligent bullet that took him off. A lady at Winchester said to us, "Ashby is a *devoted* man; this war has well nigh broken his heart."   ALTAMONT.

JESSIE SCOUTS.

When General Fremont took charge of the Mountain Department, he proceeded to follow his notion derived from experience in the Western frontier. He knew that the safety and efficiency of his army in a wild wooded and rugged region, depended upon the accuracy with which he received information of the plans and movements of the enemy.

He at once called around him a set of Western frontiersmen, who had served all through the campaign in Missouri. Some had been in the border wars of Kansas; some had served long years on the plains, hunting the buffalo and the Indian; men accustomed to every form of hardship, thoroughly skilled, not only in the use of the rifle, but drilled in all cunning ways and devices to discover the intentions, position, and strength of a foe. The best of these men were selected and placed in a small organization called the Jessie Scouts.

Their name is taken from General Fremont's wife, who remained with her husband until his army reached New Creek, Virginia. During her stay she frequently saw these men, and became very popular with them. Hence their present attachment to her. They swear by her, and wear her initials upon their coats, inserted in very modest but coarse style. They are not made prominent or ostentatiously conspicuous. The men—and I have talked with a number of them—seem equally devoted to Fremont himself. Their number when full is twenty-four.

Three of them have recently been taken, and three have been detached for service in Halleck's Department. Hence they number for some days only eighteen. They have, however, been recruiting up to the full number. One of the recent recruits whom I have seen, is a bold, dashing, fine-looking young man, a son of Brigadier General Kelly, who has been in service in Virginia for more than a year. He, therefore, has had frontier experience enough to qualify him for the undertaking. He certainly possesses the pluck. Doubtless he inherited that. Their Captain, by the way, a most remarkable character in this line of business, is Charles Carpenter, of Kansas. Born in Ohio, he went, at the age of 16, to the border of Missouri. Then (1854,) Kansas was wild and comparatively unsettled. He at once, with the ardor of his character, entered upon a wild, roving life. He has tried his hand at everything—hunting, farming, roaming, fighting Indians, Missouri border ruffians, and occasionally "Jay-hawking." He was at one time with Montgomery, at another with Jennison, and again with Cleveland. He left the last named, because, as he terms it, "things began to get too heavy even for him; he has yet some 'bowels of compassion left."

At the opening of the war, he was employed by Fremont, and went with h m to Springfield, actively scouting during the whole of the "Hundred days." Before Fremont left St. Louis, he detected, in company with another scout, two men, who had ingeniously connected a wire, over 1,100 feet long, with the regular wire over the North Missouri Road, and took off regularly the despatches sent by Fremont to his officers in North Missouri. Through these men Price obtained information of Fremont's order to Sturgis to advance to the assistance of Mulligan at Lexington. These two men these scouts were compelled to kill ere they could get possession of the wire. Their bodies were found in the bottom of a neighboring river.

Once he entered Jeff. Thompson's camp, when he threatened to take Cape Girardeau, and cross the Mississippi River, upon a foray into Illinois. The agreeable time he spent there was luxuriated in a san-insane prison, amusing the men and officers by his curious antics and monkey tricks. For two days he drove a team for Sterling Price, leaving his lines to procure forage, taking care not to return. Taken prisoner with his present Lieutenant, Robb, back of Paducah, they were carried for some distance toward Union City.

At night, they escaped by killing three men of the guard and the proprietor of the house, a violent Secessionist. Taking their horses, and assuming the garb of Confederate soldiers, they passed by Forts Henry and Donelson without the slightest interruption. Robb's ability to forge passes was of signal use to them in reaching Louisville.

Since he has been in the valley, he has sold a horse *suspected of Secession proclivities* to a man purchasing horses for Ashby's Cavalry, and then tolled him and his horses into Fremont's camp. The purchase money, (consisting of good Confederate notes,) and two horses, were thus restored to the Union, and a candidate for promotion to a permanent residence at Fort Delaware procured.

He is bronzed, so that his neck is black by exposure to the weather and sun. The eye is light blue, and the hair dark, with an inclination to curl. The face bears a youthful appearance, but looks like thirty instead of twenty-five, the real age of Carpenter. He is not above five feet six, and of high, sinewy mould. His weight is certainly not over one hundred and thirty-five. The careless, frank, Western style of manner and address belong to him. Ready for fight, fun or frolic, he is said to have mingled with his dash and boldness a remarkable prudence and caution. These qualities, united to his almost slavish devotion to Fremont, make him and his band invaluable to that commander.

His dress consists of a pair of pantaloons of a dark earthen hue, darker than buckskin. The coat is made of the dark grey material of which frontiersmen's hunting shirts are mostly made; it is a loose sack, trimmed in the cape and sleeves with fringe, gathered in the back, immediately under the shoulders, in folds or plaits. This is bound at the waist with his pistol belt. His only arm of defence, besides the six-shooter, is a breech-loading rifle, weighing about ten pounds, and good for eight hundred yards. Such is a short outline of the career and appearance of one of the most marked and eccentric characters now in this valley, waging war for the restoration of the Union.—*Correspondence Philadelphia Inquirer.*

June 26th. Judge Charles Mason, late United States commissioner of patents, called to see me to-day. The Judge will endeavor to have me paroled or exchanged, so he says. From our window we can daily see Yankees looking through opera glasses or telescopes at us, as if we were inhuman curiosities. To burlesque them, the boys hold bottles up to their eyes as if gazing at them.

The following letter from Hon. Charles Sumner, the Massachusetts negro-worshipper, shows the intimate relations, political and social, existing between him and " Abe" Lincoln. " Birds of a feather flock together." They are two peas from the same pod :

From the New York Tribune, June 26, 1862.

SENATE CHAMBER, JUNE 5, 1862.

MY DEAR SIR : Your criticism of the President is hasty. I am confident that, if you knew him as I do, you would not make it.

Of course, the President cannot be held responsible for the malfeasances of subordinates, unless adopted, or at least tolerated by him. And I am sure that nothing unjust or ungenerous will be tolerated, much less adopted, by him.

I am happy to let you know that he has no sympathy with Stanly in his absurd wickedness, closing the schools, nor again in his other act of turning our camp into a hunting ground for slaves. He repudiates both—positively. The latter point has occupied much of his thought; and the newspapers have not gone too far in recording his repeated declarations, which I have often heard from his own lips, that slaves finding their way into the national lines are never to be re-enslaved. This is his conviction, expressed without reserve.

Could you have seen the President—as it was my privilege often—while he was considering the great questions on which he has already acted—the invitation to emancipation in the States, emancipation in the District of Columbia, and the acknowledgment of the independence of Hayti and Liberia—even your zeal would have been satisfied, for you would have felt the sincerity of his purpose to do what he could to carry forward the principles of the Declaration of Independence. His whole soul was occupied, especially by the first proposition, which was peculiarly

5

his own. In familiar intercourse with him, I remember nothing more touching than the earnestness and completeness with which he embraced this idea. To his mind it was just and beneficent, while it promised the sure end of slavery. Of course to me, who had already proposed a bridge of gold for the retreating fiend, it was most welcome. Proceeding from the President, it must take its place among the great events of history.

If you are disposed to be impatient at any seeming short-comings, think, I pray you, of what has been done in a brief period, and from the past discern the sure promise of the future. Knowing something of my convictions and of the ardor with which I maintain them, you may perhaps derive some assurance from my confidence. I say to you, therefore, stand by the administration. If need be, help it by word and act, but stand by it and have faith in it.

I wish that you really knew the President, and had heard the artless expression of his convictions on those questions which concern you so deeply. You might perhaps wish that he were less cautious, but you would be grateful that he is so true to all that you have at heart. Believe me, therefore, you are wrong, and I regret it the more because of my desire to see all our friends stand firmly together.

If I write strongly, it is because I feel strongly; for my constant and intimate intercourse with the President, beginning with the 4th of March, not only binds me peculiarly to his administration, but gives me a personal as well as a political interest in seeing that justice is done him.

Believe me, my dear sir, with much regard, ever faithfully yours.

CHARLES SUMNER.

June 27th. Subjoined is an account of the scene in Baltimore on the arrival of the Confederate prisoners taken at Kernstown, near Winchester, March 23d last ; also, an article from the " New York Express" on the " Freedom of the press :"

" FREEDOM" OF THE PRESS.

The New York Express of yesterday afternoon indulges in some courageous comments on the new rescript of the Secretary of War, putting further and more onerous restraints upon the publication of intelligence in the newspapers. We subjoin a few extracts :

" What the personal risk is remains to be seen before a court martial selected and created by the party that arrests. It is clear to see, that under such 'Law,' or rather suspension of all Law, the business of newspaper publishing, or Journalising, is as perilous as any on earth. Both the Property and the Life of the Journalist are in peril—if he chances to err, in the judgment of the War Department—from which judgment, in the matter of Property, there is no appeal, and from which court martial selected by this War Department, there is no judicial relief, if death be the sentence. Prudence, of course, forbids all comment upon these very extraordinary proceedings, beyond saying that Journalism in this country, under such martial law, must run down to what it is in Constantinople, Rome, or Vienna—that is into mere criticisms upon the opera, or the fine arts, or puffs of court movements.

" What deserves especial reprehension, is—if we may be allowed thus to criticise, with a halter around our necks,—the indulgence given such men as Wendell Phillips, to roam the country, teaching the subversion of the Constitution and the Laws,—while other men, of opposite politics, for exactly the same thing, are incarcerated in Fort Warren, Fort Lafayette, or other prisons, therefor The partiality, the inequality, the injustice of this mode of treatment are so signal, that we marvel the common sense of the President does not see this wrong of his ministers, and arrest it. Upon all such partialities, and injustice, he should remember, History is making up its record,—and that the stern Muse, which records facts, will hold him responsible for these repeated inequalities of his Ministers.

The army news,—what there is—the reader cannot be half as well informed of as are the Confederates in Richmond, who now know much better what our army is doing, than the true and loyal people of the United States. Hence, our streets are full of all sorts of gossip, and of all sorts of lies.

" It was yesterday currently reported in Wall street (says the Tribune,) that a dispatch had been received at the Navy Yard, Brooklyn, stating that the Confederate steam battery Merrimac had left Norfolk, and was seen from our vessels in Hampton Roads, just off Craney Island. We learn that the report was wholly unfounded. Doubtless it was set afloat for stock jobbing purposes."

The reports from the battle about Winchester, on Sunday, and of the skirmishes, the days preceding and succeeding, are yet so obscure as but to increase the anxiety of parties having friends and relatives on that arena. It leaks out through Harrisburg, that the Colonel killed was Colonel Murray, of the 84th Pennsylvania, in consequence of which the Legislature of that State adjourned on Monday—but who are the 14 captains and lieutenants, and the 100 soldiers, none in this quarter know.

Under the new rescript from Washington, or the practical translation of it, that copying army news is as criminal as the original publication of it—it is next to impossible to know what to publish, or what not to publish. For example, we are not exactly sure—that the publication we make of the death of the Pennsylvania Colonel is not a criminal publication of army news—as it does not reach us by the Government wire.

The newspapers in this country are to be printed, it would seem by a fresh rescript from the War Department, on rather more ticklish conditions than exist in any other country, viz:—that of " warning," " suppression," or " imprisonment"—because here, the summary court martial is to try offenders, and the execution of a drum-head court is threatened.

Well, when any of our craft come down town in the morning, it would be well to say " adieu" to wife and family,—for it is not at all certain, under this rescript, that one may not be shot under drum-head law before night.

The proper way to put a stop to the publication of war news, is to cut off the mails for a few days—and shut up all the channels of intelligence. But under this rescript, a journalist is completely in the power of what, or what not, may be set down as the publication of army news.

This sort of departmental fulmination, is, to say the least, as much without decorum as without precedent. The offenders should be named, and dealt with—while this is but a fulmination in terrorem.

The above is all very good and sensible, but our cotemporary is really silly enough to quote an obsolete instrument called the Constitution of the United States, about " free speech," abridging the press, redress of grievances, etc., etc. We must, however, do it the justice to say that it adds :

" But cui bono? Why thus vainly parade Constitutions and the Civil Law ? We are struggling—(are we not?—answer, Free Speech Abolitionists!) for the emancipation of four million of Blacks,—but at what cost, Abolitionists? THE ENSLAVEMENT OF 20,000,000 OF WHITES, are we not?"

It is scarcely invidious, in this connection, to remind our friends of the Express that the independent journals of this city have long since become used to this "gag" business ; and we think, so far as the Constitution and personal liberty are concerned, they went out of use about the time of the Merryman habeas corpus case ? Did not the Express approve and sanction the action of the President in that case? We do not remember that it ever condemned the suppression of the press in this city. If, therefore, it has itself fallen into the same coils, may we not enjoy its " wry faces" with something of the relish we should those of a physician who is forced to take his own medicine?

We find the following, pertinent to the same subject, in the Boston Post.

The Washington correspondent of the New York Evening Post says:

" Free speech and free press is something which is not yet fully understood by pro-slavery men in this vicinity."

We should think they might understand "something" about them after reading the report of the Judiciary Committee on the censorship of the Press, as practiced by the Post's political friends, or by conversing with editors whose papers were denied transportation in the mails, or by conversing with men suspected of having said " something" not agreeable to certain officials, and who have been imprisoned without accusation or trial.

ARRIVAL OF CONFEDERATE PRISONERS—THEY ARE CONSIGNED TO THE CITY JAIL.

VISITORS DENIED ADMISSION.

Shortly before 5 o'clock yesterday afternoon a special train arrived at the Camden Station, from Sandy Hook, near Harper's Ferry, having on board 236 Confederate prisoners, said to have been captured in and about Winchester, Va., in charge of company B, 4th Ohio regiment, Captain Bourning.

No notice had been given that the prisoners were expected, and the fact was not generally known, but immediately upon the arrival of the train, and in fact before it had fairly entered the depot, the news became circulated, and spread like wildfire. The crowd around the depot rapidly increased, and in a very short time the train was completely surrounded by persons all anxious to catch a glimpse of the strangers ; some out of morbid curiosity, but a majority being desirous of grasping them by the hands, or searching among the crowd for some familiar face.

Leaving the depot, they filed into Howard street, and took up the line of march to the quarters provided for them, at the City Hall. As they passed up Howard street, the passers-by thronged the sidewalks and street corners, and the ladies, with that independence which characterizes the Baltimore ladies, waved their handkerchiefs to the prisoners, which was politely acknowledged by them, and many raised their hats and returned the salutation with beaming faces and smiles of heartfelt thanks for the sympathy expressed.

The demand for cakes, apples, refreshments, and everything in the shape of edibles, was astonishing. In a very few minutes the entire stock on hand about the depot was bought up by those assembled, who distributed them freely among the unfortunate soldiers.

A large force of police soon arrived in charge of Marshal James L. McPhail, and the crowd was forced back from the cars to enable them to disembark. They were formed in line two abreast, the Federal soldiers and the police flanking them upon either side. As they passed out of the depot, the multitude, which had increased to several thousand, pressed forward, and shook hands with many of them, expressing sympathy for them in their misfortune.

Many of the dwellings along the route presented a lively appearance, as the windows were occupied by men, women, and children, many of them waving hats and handkerchiefs; others, however, gave vent to their feelings by hooting, hissing, and giving vent to all sorts of disapprobation ; some exclaiming, "There's a specimen of your Southern chivalry ;" "Oh, what a set of ragamuffins," &c. The prisoners looked defiance at them, however, and treated all such, who so expressed themselves, with the utmost contempt.

Passing into Madison street, they proceeded towards the jail, followed by an immense crowd. When near the jail building, a citizen living in the vicinity appeared at his window, with several children, who shouted vociferously for Jeff. Davis, whereupon several of the prisoners turned towards them, and became so excited as to take up the shout, and, despite the presence of the armed guard, cheered for Jeff. Davis with a hearty good will, raising their caps to those in the windows.

The crowd caught the infection, and shouts of "Go it boys; them's my sentiments ;" "We ain't all Yankees here, nary a time ; "We're with you if we had a chance ;" and similar exclamations were heard. Arriving at the jail gate, the crowd made another rush to get an opportunity to shake hands, but were pressed back, and the prisoners were marched inside the jail building and delivered over to Captain James, who provided them with quarters in the northern corridor of the building.

The outside gate was soon besieged by a large number of people, all claiming the right to enter upon various pretexts. Quite a number did obtain ingress, and conversed freely with the prisoners, who seemed quite communicative and gratified at the attention paid to them.

A majority of them are very young men and are very intelligent. A great many present the appearance of being farmers and laborers, many of whom state that they were only "Home Guards," and not attached to the regular army, and were captured at their homes, and not in the battle at Winchester. Of this, however, we know nothing, except that the Federals claim them as prisoners of war. They are nearly all from the neighborhood of Staunton, Va. So far as we have been able to learn there are no Baltimoreans among them, as reported. They are a very hardy looking body of men, but rather rough in outward appearance, having doubtless been in active service for several months past. The uniforms, which are of grey, are warm and comfortable.

They were provided last evening with refreshments by the gentlemanly warden of the jail, Captain James, who renders them as comfortable as circumstances will admit.

At an early hour this morning numbers of persons assembled at the jail to obtain an interview, and among them many of the first ladies of the city, who were anxious to relieve their wants, but an order was received to close the gates, and all communication even to the press was denied. We are informed, however, that any packages of clothing or delicacies sent to them will be delivered to them by the authorities. Among the party are eighteen non-commissioned officers, who are very intelligent and gentlemanly, and all of whom seem thoroughly wrapt up heart and soul in the Southern cause.

I am more and more disgusted every day at the very sight of dark blue uniforms—in proportion to my attachment to the South, is my indignant wrath at her enemies. Let us have no terms to make with the hordes and vandals who seek to destroy us by the most unscrupulous and barbarous warfare the world has ever known. Would that I had the power to scatter them like chaff with the breath of my mouth!

June 29th. It is generally believed by the prisoners that we have badly whipped the Yankees before Richmond. Yankee newspapers try to conceal it, but their conflicting accounts of battles betray their efforts to pervert the truth. May it be so, and if so, *Deo Gracias!* The Yankee officers here say that General McClellan is certainly on "Church Hill."

June 30th. The editor of the "Baltimore American" has been arrested, it is said, for publishing the accounts of the battles before Richmond *too soon.* Having met with the subjoined address, I record it as a part of the current history of the times:

Address of the Democratic Members of Congress to the Democracy of the United States.

FELLOW-CITIZENS :—The perilous condition of our country demands that we should reason together. Party organization, restricted within proper limits, is a positive good, and indeed essential to the preservation of public liberty. Without it the best government would soon degenerate into the worst of tyrannies. In despotisms the chief use of power is in crushing out party opposition. In our country the experience of the past twelve months proves, more than any lesson in history, the necessity of party organization. The present administration was chosen by a party, and in all civil acts and appointments has recognized, and still does, its fealty and obligations to that party. *There must and will be an opposition.* The public safety and

good demand it. The Democratic party was founded more than
sixty years ago. It has never been disbanded. To-day it numbers one million five hundred thousand electors in the States still
loyal to the Union. Its recent numerous victories in municipal
elections in the Western and Middle States proves its vitality.
Within the last ten months it has held State Conventions, and
nominated full Democratic tickets in every free State in the
Union. Of no other party opposed to the Republicans can the
same be said. Shall the Democratic party be now disbanded ?
Why should it ? Are its ancient principles wrong ? What are
they ? Let its platforms for thirty years speak :

"*Resolved*, That the American Democracy place their trust
in the intelligence, the patriotism, and the discriminating justice of the American people. That we regard this as a distinc-
tive feature in our political creed, which we are proud to main
tain before the world, as the great moral element in a form of
government, springing from and upheld by the popular will ;
and we contrast it with the creed and practice of Federalism,
under whatever name and form which seeks to palsy the will of
the constituent, and which conceives no imposture too mon-
strous for the public credulity. "That the Federal Government is one of limited power, derived *solely* from the constitution, and the grants of power made therein ought to be strictly
construed by all the departments and agents of the government; and that it is *inexpedient* and *dangerous* to exercise doubtful constitutional powers.

And as explanatory of these the following from Mr. Jefferson's inaugural : "The support of the State Governments in
all their rights as the most complete administration of our domestic concerns, and the surest bulwarks against anti-Republi-
can tendencies. The preservation of the General Government
in its whole constitutional vigor, as the sheet anchor of our peace
at home and safety abroad." Such, Democrats, are the principles of your party, essential to public liberty, and to the sta-
bility and wise administration of the government, alike in peace
and war. They are the principles upon which the Constitution
and Union were founded ; and under the control of a party
which adheres to them, the constitution would be maintained,
and the Union could not be dissolved.

This morning Lieutenant Holmes (one of the Yankee officers) came up to our room and enquired "who has been talking to a man outside through the bars ?" "No one in this
room," was the reply, when he went out, looking as if he
believed we were falsifying. Soon Lieutenant Holmes, or

" Mullet-head," as the " boys" call him, returned and said, " I have the *culprit*. The gentleman on the street to whom the prisoner was talking was arrested, and the prisoner himself put in solitary confinement. Some two weeks ago two little girls were arrested for waving their handkerchiefs to prisoners, and a little child who could not speak plainly for saying "Hoowaugh for Bowaygard."

July 2d. A little girl, 12 years of age, was arrested to-day for wearing an apron like the Confederate flag. The surgeon of this prison is known as " Cyclops" among us. A week ago "Cyclops" said " our forces are about now in Richmond—the Anaconda is gradually coiling around the last vital point of the rebellious monster." What does he think now ? The " New York Times" acknowledges the loss of upwards of twenty pieces of artillery in one fight. The Yankee papers a week ago reported General Thomas C. Hindman, of Arkansas, as certainly dead.

In yesterday's paper is the following telegram :—" Advices from Arkansas are to the effect that General Hindman, with some five thousand rebels, was in the immediate vicinity of the St. Charles," and that Colonel Fitch had abandoned the forts, spiking the guns. The situation of General Curtis is said to be critical, he being unable to obtain supplies, and his army having been on half rations for a week :

THE FATE OF RICHMOND.

We expected to have been able to announce in our yesterday afternoon's edition the important fact that Richmond was in possession of General McClellan's army. From sources of information which we deemed trustworthy, we, however, believe that the fact was known in this city yesterday afternoon, and also communicated by the authorities here to Washington, but for reasons no doubt satisfactory, an official recognition of the fact was withheld by the War Department. Our theory of the case is this: Although the city is in our power or possession, yet the Rebel army is still in arms, but is so situated that it can neither escape from the coils of the anaconda with which McClellan enfolds it, nor has it the means of obtaining supplies; neither can it attack our forces, who hold the possession of the bridges over the Chickahominy, which are controlled by our heavy artillery, and there is no other means of access to McClellan, it being impossible for the Rebels to get through the marshes adjacent to the river. The result must be that the Rebels must surrender or starve, as they can neither fight or skedaddle. They are in a *fix*

This, as before remarked, is our theory of the matter, and the government withholds the official intelligence of the taking of Richmond, until it can accompany it with the additional gratifying announcement, which probably they may be able to make in time to send to England by the steamer which sails to-day, of the capture not only of Richmond, but of the entire Rebel army. For giving this *opinion*, we hope we may not be called upon to keep our neighbor company at Fort McHenry.—*Baltimore Clipper, July 2.*

July 3d. Parson Brownlow, of Tennessee, delivered a speech last night at Ford's Atheneum, in this city, to a large audience.

The meeting closed with lusty cheers for the Parson, State of Tennessee, and the Union:

Extracts from Northern papers.

FUGITIVE SLAVE CASE IN ALEXANDRIA.

We take the following particulars of a slave case in Alexandria, Virginia, from the News of June 24 :

John Hunter, a citizen of Prince George county, in the State of Maryland, applied to Lewis McKenzie, a justice of the peace of Alexandria county, Virginia, for a warrant to arrest certain slaves of his, supposed to be in this city. Having taken and subscribed the following oath, required before the magistrate would grant a warrant :

State of Virginia, Alexandria County : I, John Hunter, of the county of Prince George, in the State of Maryland, do solemnly swear that I am a true and loyal citizen of the United States, and that I will support the constitution thereof as the supreme law of the land ; and that I will, to the extent of my abilities, uphold and maintain it. I will, to the utmost of my power, give information of every danger which may threaten it, so help me God.

JOHN HUNTER.

Sworn to before me this 21st day of June, 1862.

LEWIS McKENZIE, *J. P.*

A warrant was accordingly granted, and one of Mr. Hunter's negroes, on Saturday last, was apprehended, and the officers were conveying him to the ferry boat for transportation home, there being no doubt of its being Mr. Hunter's servant from the evidence of parties present, satisfactory to the magistrate. Not pleased with the summary proceedings of the parties executing the warrant, the negro refused to accompany them, when they essayed gentle " coercion." This not meeting with the approbation of the negro, was creating some excitement, and promised to lead to serious difficulty, when some of the provost guard interposed and carried the case before Colonel Gregory, the Provost Marshal, who retained possession of the negro until the 23d, when a decision was rendered. After receiving the statements of Mayor McKenzie, Mr. Hunter and his friends, the negro and others, in connection with the report of the guard, the Marshal refused to acknowledge the claim of Mr. Hunter, and released the man, stating that he would not permit the arrest of any fugitive from labor while in command of this post, thus setting aside the lawful authority of the State of Virginia. The case will be reported to the President at an early day.

A SECESSIONIST.

A friend in this city tells us of a little boy, a neighbor of his, who took great pleasure in a beautiful play-ball painted with our own national colors. While enjoying his play on the sidewalk recently, the ball accidentally rolled into a neighbor's basement. It was returned to him after a while, with the red, white and blue washed off, and a Secesh flag painted on instead. Comment is needless.

A gentleman from Chicago relates a remarkable fact in connection with the Rebel prisoners at Chicago. The Rebel prisoners number about eight thousand, and, of course, there are among them men of intelligence and education, but the great numbers are deplorably ignorant. Colonel Mulligan has these Rebels in charge, and as they have considerable leisure time, he has established a Yankee school for their instruction. The educated prisoners were assigned as teachers, and the work is progressing rapidly

Two discharged members of the fourteenth regiment of regulars, who have just arrived at Syracuse, New York, from Perryville, Maryland, state that about the first of last February the Rebel sympathizers in that town poisoned the wells, from which the men were in the habit of procuring their drinking water, and that, as a consequence, two hundred members of the regiment died, and of the remaining seven hundred, hardly one has recovered his health.

Mr. Wm. P Wood, superintendent, informed us this evening that the prisoners here will be removed to Fort Delaware on to-morrow.

July 4th. Captain Higgins and Lieutenant J. Miller have treated us since our confinement here with comparative kindness, and all the prisoners have become somewhat attached to them on that account. Their conduct towards us has been a pleasing contrast with the uncouth bearing and tyranny in petty things of other officers. The following will explain itself.

At a meeting held this morning, in room No. 3, the following preamble and resolution were unanimously adopted :

" Whereas Captain Benjamin D. Higgins and Lieutenant J. Miller (as officers connected with this prison) have by their gentlemanly, courteous and soldierly bearing towards us, won our esteem and respect,

Therefore, be it Resolved, That it is with regret that we part with these gentlemen, inasmuch as they have exemplified that urbane and respectful bearing, even in our present relations with each other, is not incompatible with the faithful discharge of a soldier's duty."

Captain E. Pliny Bryan was called to the chair, and a committee of three was appointed to hand these resolutions to the above named.

About half past 10, A. M., we started in charge of Lieutenant J. B. Mix, of " Scott's nine hundred," for the depot, where we were detained an hour. United States soldiers and citizens crowded around the cars. Beyond the expressions of a few intoxicated men, nothing insulting was said to us, but great anxiety was manifested to converse with us, which, in every instance, was prohibited. Several persons, however, stepped up under the windows of the cars, covered their mouths with their hands, and said in an under tone, "I'm Secesh, and sympathize with you." One, while he did this, dropped two gold dollars into the hands of a prisoner, enquiring audibly, " How are you, brother Jim ?" A lady requested the officer in charge to allow her to speak to her *cousin,* and she was permitted to do so. Her cousin, Lieutenant S., then received from her a card, on which was written the name of a lady he had known in Charleston, South Carolina. In return he handed her a card, on which was a likeness of President Davis, and she seemed delighted at the exchange. On the departure of the train from the depot, the prisoners vociferously cheered for Davis, Beauregard and John-ston. Arrived in Baltimore at 2, P M. As we moved along the streets in the same cars, drawn by horses to the Philadel-phia depot, the prisoners sang Southern songs, and cheered for Davis, while men and women, concealed behind obstacles and windows, were seen to waive handkerchiefs at them. Notwith-standing the array of bayonets and swords, down-trodden South-ern feeling was thus made apparent. At this time a Confederate Lieutenant hallooed for Beauregard, and a Yankee officer re-plied, " D—n Beauregard, I wish he was in h—ll, where you ought to be." As we advanced towards Philadelphia, we found the Secession feeling growing less. Passing a small town in Pennsylvania, a " Louisiana Tiger" cried out, " Hurrah for Jackson," and a woman replied, " Go to h—ll." At Havre de Grace, in Maryland, the " tiger" above mentioned, displayed a small Confederate flag, whereupon an overgrown inebriated fellow said, " I can whip the man that showed that flag if the officer in charge will let us have a fair open fight." The officer took the flag away from the " tiger," and told the man, in a joke, that he might " have a fair open fight," but the man, I sup-pose, thought discretion the better part of valor, for he declined to accept the privilege. Lieutenant J B. Mix, the officer in charge, proved himself a very clever gentleman, and did all he could to make us as comfortable as circumstances would allow. We arrived in Philadelphia at 12 o'clock at night. As late as it was a small crowd had collected at the depot, and there was a great disposition manifested to talk with us—some few seemed inclined to talk rationally and calmnly, while others made this an occasion to vent their venom freely, which latter invariably recoiled upon them with " good measure pressed down, heaped up and running over." Had not an officer interfered, they would have torn a Louisianian " to pieces," as they said. An old woman remarked, " My husband and three sons are before Richmond, and I wish I had more to send. I wish they would let me kill them rebels. Why don't they kill 'em?" Many loose remarks were made, such as " they have no free schools, and are so ignorant," " they want a monarchy," &c., &c. Lieuten-ant Mix went to get us something to eat at a restaurant, but was refused, the keeper saying he would sell nothing to rebels, and he hoped we would starve. Some of the people said that the " Southerners" treated their prisoners very badly, which was stoutly denied. Mr. Olden from Aldie, Virginia, told them that he was kept four days handcuffed without anything to eat, and the crowd agreed that " he ought not to have had anything to eat—any man that would turn traitor to his country." In a conversation with a Federal officer the latter was frank enough to say that he wished we had peace ; he was tired of the war ; would resign if he could do so without disgrace ; that if the North backed down now, they would be a ruined and a disgraced people, and that they were fighting for their very existence.

At 5 o'clock we left Philadelphia for Fort Delaware, which is forty miles south-west of " the city of brotherly love ?" We were evidently brought this circuitous rout for display—to lead the people to believe we were prisoners from Richmond. Arrived at the fort at 10 o'clock, A. M.—a gloomy looking place. At the west end of the fort the roll was called immediately on our entrance in the yard. As the names were called the officers were ordered inside the fort, and the non-commissioned officers and privates to an enclosure like a sheep-pen. Captain A. Gibson, commandant of the post, seemed to endeavor by harsh expressions and manner to intimidate the prisoners. Assuming as much ferocity as possible, he would say, " Why don't you answer to your name, sir ?" " Speak louder, walk along faster," &c., &c. ; but he always had thrust back at him as harsh language as he could adopt. A Louisianian, after replying " here," in a stentorian voice, as his name was called, *gave old Gibson a look of vengeance,* and the latter remarked, " A damned impudent scoundrel." Lieutenant Mix, (the officer in charge of the prisoners from Washington to Fort Delaware,) told us that the train in which we came to Philadelphia was expected at the latter place four hours earlier than it arrived, and that had we been up to time, we would probably have been mobbed, for about two thousand had assembled and waited an hour at the depot for us for that purpose. As it was, two of the prisoners were struck with rocks, one on the head, and the other in the side.

July 6th. Our monotonous confinement furnishes but little worthy of record, but memory leads me back to our experience at the Philadelphia depot ; and I laugh at what was said and done by the bitter and misguided fanatics. An old woman came up under the car window and asked Captain S. very seriously, " When will this war end ?" to which the Captain replied, " Madam, when all of your troops are withdrawn from our soil"— a man who standing by, who had been boring us for some time with his Bombastes Furiosi talk, said to Captain S., " I wish I had you out of the cars, I'd take your heart out"—this same man had the impudence to try to draw Major H. into conversation with him, but the latter told him, " I want nothing to say to you—you insulted my friend, and you might insult me," and the man walked off like a dog with his tail between his legs. A pleasant-looking fellow, with a seemingly inexhaustible flask of whiskey in his pocket, and good humor issuing from every pore of his jolly countenance, was passing from car to car, (while we were waiting so long at the Philadelphia depot,) and discussing with evident satisfaction to himself the great question which divided the late "United States." At length we all became heartily tired of his witticisms, and one after another "poohed" and "pshawed" at him. At this he became very angry, and began to use Billingsgate language pretty freely, but throughout his antics he came off No. 2.

July 7th. The New York Herald attempts to prove Horace Greely a Secessionist, by quotations from his own paper :

From the Tribune of November 9, 1860.

If the cotton States shall become satisfied that they can do better out of the Union than in it, we insist on letting them go in peace. The right to secede may be a revolutionary one; but it exists, nevertheless. * * * We must ever resist the right of any State to remain in the Union and nullify or defy the laws thereof. To withdraw from the Union is quite another matter; and whenever a considerable section of our Union shall deliberately resolve to go out, we shall resist all coercive measures designed to keep it in. We hope never to live in a Republic whereof one section is pinned to another by bayonets.

From the Tribune of November 26, 1860.

If the cotton States unitedly and earnestly wish to withdraw peacefully from the Union, we think they should and would be allowed to do so. Any attempt to compel them by force to remain would be contrary to the principles enunciated in the immortal Declaration of Independence, contrary to the fundamental ideas on which human liberty is based.

From the Tribune of December 17, 1860.

If it (the Declaration of Independence) justified the secession from the British empire of three millions of colonists in 1776, we do not see why it would not justify the secession of five millions of Southerners from the Union in 1861.

From the Tribune of February 23, 1861.

We have repeatedly said, and we once more insist, that the great principle embodied by Jefferson in the Declaration of American Independence, that governments derive their just power from the consent of the governed, is sound and just; and that, if the slave States, the cotton States, or the Gulf States only, choose to form an independent nation, they have a clear moral right to do so. * * * * Whenever it shall be clear that the great body of the Southern people have become conclusively alienated from the Union, and anxious to escape from it, we shall do our best to forward their views.

July 18th. There is said to be about 3,000 prisoners confined at this fort, the majority of which are in a pen, which is called "the barracks," and which I shall more fully describe hereafter. The men sleep two on a board, about three feet wide—are compelled to cut their hair short—are marched and countermarched about an hour every day—felt all over by the Dutch sergeants, and made to bring water and do other work about the garrison. They have "coffee-water" sometimes, and a piece of bread six by three inches, and a small piece of meat scarcely fit for a dog to eat, for breakfast; "soup-water" for dinner, with bread about the dimensions above, and "coffee-water for supper, and bread same as at breakfast and dinner. They drink river water, which is really offensive to the smell. The privy they use is intolerably filthy, and accommodation for three thousand is not large enough for three hundred.

A Yankee soldier who attempted to escape from this fort, where he was on duty, was sentenced to carry the ball and chain four hours every day for five months! He has been carrying it three months now. I see the poor fellow every day from my window, and he appears to be in much suffering. The following, in regard to this fort, is from the "Philadelphia Enquirer."

FORT DELAWARE AND THE REBEL PRISONERS.—There are, at the present time, 3,181 rebel prisoners confined at Fort Delaware, and about 3,000 more expected at the end of next week. The steamer Baltic arrived at the Fort on Saturday last, having on board 1,200 prisoners, who were transferred from Governor's Island, New York, to Fort Delaware; they comprise the whole number quartered at Governor's Island. The rumors of an outbreak recently of the prisoners at the Fort have no foundation in fact. While it is conceded by officers of the Fort that a determined attempt at capture would create trouble, no ultimate good to the rebels could possibly result.

The prisoners, with the exception of the rebel officers, who are about one hundred in number, and who have quarters inside the Fort, occupy barracks on the upper end of the Island. These barracks are commanded by heavy casemate guns in the Fort, and also by shotted field pieces. A strong guard also patrols the Island at all hours, to prevent any attempt at escape. The barracks erected are capable of accommodating 2,000 men. Other barracks are in course of erection, intended to accommodate 5,000 more. The guard consists of about 250 men, comprising portions of three batteries.

Recruiting is going on in this city to fill these batteries to the required standard, and with flattering success. Lieutenant Wm. G. Rohrman is employed in this service, and a considerable number are recruited and sent down daily. The troops are encamped on the meadows near the Fort. One company, numbering about sixty men and about thirty regulars, are stationed inside. A hospital has been built near the barracks for the sick and wounded rebels, and every attention given to them.

Extracts from proceedings in the United States House of Representatives.

Mr. Mallory, of Kentucky. I think the slaves of Southern rebels should be used as our armies advance in all menial service, such as boating and assisting in the fortifications. My reasons against arming them are—1st. That when armed they would be turned against those who had been their masters, and their practice will be an indiscriminate slaughter of men, women and children. 2d. You cannot for your lives make of slaves an army whose services in the field will pay the expense of organizing them. One shot from a cannon would disperse thirty thousand of them.

Mr. Stevens, of Pennsylvania. Then they will do injury to the rebels who fight them. I am for employing them against their masters. I suppose the gentleman wants to employ the slaves in a menial service, and after the war return them to their masters under the fugitive slave law. I would raise 100,000 to-morrow. They are not barbarians, and are as much calculated to be humane as any class of people. It is false to say they will not make good soldiers. I would seize every foot of land and dollar of property, and apply them to the army as we go along. I would plant in the South military colonies, and sell the land to soldiers of freedom, holding the heritage of traitors; and building up institutions without the recognition of slavery.

Mr. Wickliffe, of Kentucky. It is a miserable policy to muster runaway blacks into service. If twenty million of freemen cannot suppress a rebellion of six millions of white men, let the acknowledgment at once be made.

July 9th. On the 4th of July President Davis, dressed in full regimentals, after the ceremony of a mock trial, was hung in effigy in west Philadelphia.

A prisoner, attached to a Virginia regiment, was taken sick last night, and carried from the barracks to the hospital *at 9 o'clock, and was buried at* 10 *o'clock.* Quick work !

I shall have been here a week the day after to-morrow. We are so closely confined that it seems like a month on account of the " weary, lagging hours." A fellow prisoner says he has been here a month, and he has to write 1862 every day, so as not to forget it, for it appears like 1863.

July 10th. One of the modes adopted here, in order to tantalize us, is to tell us we " are to be paroled or exchanged tomorrow." This once had the effect to fill the prisoners with the roseate hues of hope, but disappointment had so often been the result of such announcements, that we no longer listen to them with credit.

The Yankees certainly do not desire the release of Colonel Corcoran, nor have they ever desired it. His confinement appeals too strongly to the Irish to volunteer, and about this time particularly volunteers are much needed.

Mr. Fessenden, of Maine, said in the Senate yesterday, " There is another thing I think a great mistake, and that is the attempt to deceive the people by calling a defeat "a great strategetic movement." He thought the people should be trusted, and told the whole truth as to what was wanted by the country. Deal with them honestly, and every true Northern heart will respond, deal with enemies as enemies, and friends as friends. It is folly to hesitate to tell the people of this country exactly what the state of things is. He had been amused by seeing a call upon the different Governors for 300,000 troops, which simply meant that the President and Government thought they would want more troops. The enemy knows this, everybody knows it, then why not tell the truth?

Mr. Rice, Senator from Minnesota, said: "The time had come when we must either recognise the Southern Confederacy, or speedily put it down—use all the means in our power to do so. Must we, when the rebels resort to all sorts of means, fail from any sickly notions, and refrain from using all the means in our power to meet and suppress the rebellion? He would not hesitate for a moment to vote for any measure that would put the rebellion to an end."

Mr. Wilson, of Massachusetts, was in favor of fighting the battle to a successful issue, and drafting if necessary, but he agreed with the Senator from Maine that this style of rose-water must cease, that it would be better to tell the whole truth to the people, and not attempt to deceive them. *It seemed as if we had an organized system of lying in this country.* "He thought the censorship of the press had been a great disadvantage."

Most of the articles in the newspapers in reference to the war are simply malicious falsehoods, the creation of base minds and evil hearts.

The Washington correspondent of the Philadelphia Enquirer says: "Lieutenant Clure, of the 92d Ohio, with 28 rebel prisoners from the Shenandoah Valley, arrived to-day, and while en route to the Provost Marshal's office they were taken to a Secession house on C street, and feasted for several hours, and then taken to a number of drinking saloons by Secesh sympathizers"

July 11th. Joseph C. Paul, a private in Company K, Pennsylvania Zouaves, says in a letter dated James river, July 5th, to a friend in Philadelphia, "We are now lying near James river, and rest assured that if the enemy attack us again before we are prepared, it will not be a loss of five nights' sleep to us as before, as we will occupy Richmond as sure as fate. This is the opinion of distinguished officers."

Lincoln has gone on a visit to the army of the Potomac, accompanied by P. H. Watson, assistant Secretary of War.

The "Philadelphia Evening Bulletin" says General Burnside has promptly brought his fine division of veterans, who have won laurels at Roanoke Island and Newbern, to James river, and they are now joined to the army of the Potomac."

Captain Gibson tells us to-day that arrangements have been made for an immediate exchange of prisoners.

The Philadelphia Enquirer says, "Major Trumbull, of the first Connecticut artillery, has arrived in town, and is fast recovering from an attack of the Chickahominy fever." It is presumed that the Major referred to is not the only one suffering from the Chickahominy fever about this time.

July 12th. Gold is riz, and, in the language of the poet, it threatens to be rizzer. Some Yankee financiers argue that gold is not up, but that paper is down! This question between pecuniary tweedledee and tweedledum seems to puzzle the *quid nuncs* since the retreat of McClellan.

A sergeant escaped from the barracks last night. He lives in Baltimore. To all intents and purposes Captain Gibson, in command of this post, is a prisoner on the island, whose only consolation seems to be to exercise his petty tyranny over "rebel" prisoners. There are men whose nature has a peculiar affinity for anything petty, mean, and bad. They fly upon it like a vulture upon carrion. I discover that it is the policy of the Yankees to allow those in immediate attendance on the inmates of prisons to *seem* to grant them some indulgences *at times*, in order to gain their confidence, and arrive at their secrets. Some ladies from Delaware visited the Fort yesterday, and when concealed behind pillars, so as not to be seen by the officers of the Fort, they waved their handkerchiefs at the prisoners. After they left, they sent a request, clandestinely, to them for "Secession buttons." The ladies, as a general thing, North and South, seem to be with us. This speaks well for the *heart* of the Southern people, for this is the commodity ladies deal in.

July 13th. From Yankee newspapers it seems that gold has become scarce, since it has risen so in value:

The Gold and the Silver
Have vanished and fled,
And people must carry
Shinplasters instead.

A gentleman from Florida, who has been a prisoner at Fort Lafayette, in New York harbor, was brought here yesterday. At Fort Layfayette he has been in double irons since the 27th of April last, because it was alleged that he was a captain of a band of guerillas to hang Union men. He is a private attached to the 3d Florida regiment, Colonel Dilworth. The Yankees have threatened to hang him several times. He was captured at St. Johns, while within an hundred yards of his house, whither he was going on furlough. A sermon was preached in the Fort this evening, and my friend Lieutenant W., who has fortunately a religious turn of mind, heard it, and informs me that it was a fine effort, although emanating from a Yankee.

The gist of it was that religion is not incompatible with a soldier's life. For my own part, I believe that as no good can come out of Nazareth, or pure water from a foul spring, so nothing sincere can fall from a Yankee's lips.

Look at "Old Gip" (Captain Gibson) as he winds about the yard of the fort! His slim figure is made all the slimmer by tight pantaloons. He walks with as quick a step as his left leg twisted at an angle of forty-seven degrees will permit. He carries his chin as if conscious of a stiff cravat, and his old palm leaf hat is set with a knowing inclination to the left ear. "Old Gip" is a tall, spare and ungainly looking man, of about fifty years of age, with a pale ascetic countenance, which carries with it an expression vibrating between low suspicion and vulgarity. His hair is cut tolerably close, close enough to display in their full proportions a large pair of ears, which stand out in "relief" like turrets from a watch-tower, and with pretty much the same object. His beard is short, and of pepper and salt color, and he has a malicious twinkling eye. Most persons have some prevailing characteristic, which usually gives tone and color to all their thoughts and actions, forming what we denominate *temperament*. The temperament of "Old Gip" seems to take delight in being as rough, uncouth, and disobliging as possible to all whom cruel fate has brought with the unfortunate limits of his tyranny. Occasionally the officers are allowed to walk on the parapet of the fort for recreation for about an half hour. Any conversation with the sentinels is strictly forbidden, and for not observing the rule in this respect, some officers have been placed in solitary confinement. Not long since, while the Confederate officers were walking on the parapet, they noticed a vessel approaching with a flag, which, at a distance, looked exactly like the Confederate flag, and the conversation became general upon the subject, in the course of which, one of the officers observed, in a jocular way, that he believed it was the "stars and bars," and said, "Hurrah for Jeff Davis." Soon the sentinel informed us, "Your time is up," and we had scarcely reached our quarters when the officer above referred to received a note from "Old Gip," in which the Yankee functionary used this language: "For this, your first offence, I *warn* you, but for a repetition of the crime, may God have mercy on your soul!" The sentinel must have informed Captain Gibson of the *crime*, for the latter was not within hearing when the remark was made.

July 14th. An old Dutch soldier in the fort said to-day, " I don't care which side whips by Got, so I gets my thirteen dollars a month." Another Yankee soldier remarked to a prisoner, "You have plenty of friends in this yard, but we must keep

7

mum." Captain Gibson has just issued an order preventing pri-soners from receiving money from their friends, but allows them to buy necessaries from the sutler, and give an order on him when he has funds in his hands belonging to a prisoner. This is caused by the escape of several prisoners lately, for it is supposed that the sentinels were bribed by the parties who escaped.

The Black Republican members of the United States Congress are as far from mixing with the Democrats as oil with water. The two are always quarrelling in spite of the fact, that the Black Re-publicans are ever trying to be a little more Democratic, while the Democrats make constant efforts to be a little "Republican." In this way the Black Republicans are like onions rubbed with De-mocratic spices ; the strong original nigger odor is blended with new and foreign matter. However much the Democrats aim to conceal the fact, it is quite plain that Black Republican Onion offends Democratic nostrils, while the new Democratic spice is quite unwelcome to the genuine Black Republican.

July 15th. Ten prisoners escaped last night. From a North-ern paper I learn that the following dispatch has just been received at the War Department, "Nashville," July 14th. It was the ninth, instead of the eleventh Michigan regiment, that surrendered at Murfreesboro', Tennessee. The eleventh arrived at the camp near the Davisville Fair Grounds, yesterday afternoon, after an un-successful three days' chase after Morgan. Three members of Hewitt's battery, who escaped from Murfreesboro', report that the battery and the third Minnesota surrendered to the rebels. Colo-nel Duffield is mortally wounded, and General T A. Crittenden, of Indiana, taken prisoner.

Mrs. Phillips, who was not long since released from the old ca-pitol prison at Washington city, and sent South, has been again arrested by an order from "Beast Butler," on the charge of "mocking" at the funeral remains of Lieutenant De Kay, and imprisoned in one of the houses on Ship Island, intended for hos-pital purposes, where she is to be allowed one female servant, and no more, and a soldier's ration a day, with the means of cooking it. Another order from the same source sentences Fidel Keller or Kelti to two years' hard labor on Ship Island for exhibiting in his bookstore window a skeleton labelled "Chickahominy." A third order sentences John W Audins to hard labor for two years, for having exhibited a cross, which he said was fashioned from the bones of a Yankee soldier.

Lincoln has just had an interview with the members of Con-gress from the border States, the object of which is said to have been to impress upon them the necessity of urging their respec-tive States to adopt the gradual emancipation policy, in order to avoid, says the New York Express, "immediate and bloody abo-lition." The telegraph reports that General Curtis, (who is endeavoring to retreat through Arkansas to the Mississippi river, opposite Memphis,) is suffering terribly for want of forage and supplies. Also, on Monday, his command was at Jacksonport, and General Hindman had ordered the railroad bridge at Madison to be burned, to prevent Curtis from passing in that direction, and had also required all the inhabitants near Gauley bridge to burn their provisions and shoot their cattle, lest they should be seized by foraging parties sent out by Curtis. Charges have been preferred against General Mitchell by the division formerly commanded by him in North Alabama. He is accused of having permitted a portion of his troops to perpetrate upon the people of North Alabama "deeds of cruelty and of guilt, the bare narration of which makes the heart sick." Ex-President Fillmore says "that the Abolitionists in Congress had undone what the army had done."

The New York Express says : "Adjutant General Thomas came to this city a day or two ago to make arrangements concerning Confederate prisoners at Governor's Island and Fort Lafayette. After a thorough examination, it was found inexpedient to permit any considerable number of Secessionists to occupy Governor's Island. It is one of the largest ordnance depots in the United States. The arsenal on the island contains millions of dollars worth of war material, and as the different fortifications constitute a part of our harbor defences, and the armaments constantly ready for use, a comparatively small number of Secessionists, should the guard in any event be overpowered, could do a vast amount of damage. The prisoners, numbering 1,100, have been taken to Fort Delaware." They have arrived.

July 16th. The papers report the thermometer at 90° in the shade. It must be 100° in the room in which we are confined. We are losing flesh and health rapidly. A call for a mass meeting in New Jersey says, among other things : "While the waning ranks of the rebels are furnished by conscription, let it be our boast that we defend the nation by the heroic volunteer." The New York Tribune says : "There are upwards of three thousand prisoners on that island, (Pea Patch Island,) among which is the notorious Colonel Pettigrew. Colonel Gibson, with a sufficient force at his command, has charge of the prisoners. One of the finest forts in the country is being constructed on that island. The island is located forty miles south of Philadelphia, and two and a half from the nearest point of the main land." A correspondent of the Buffalo Express, writing from Old Point Comfort, under date of July 4th, says: "The 44th, (Ellsworth Avengers,) which I persist in calling the finest regiment that ever took the field, is a mere wreck. On Wednesday, after the last of their many fights, they stacked arms with only 90 muskets—a sad remainder of the original 1,040 men. Of the greater portion, some are killed, more are wounded, and still more are home on sick leave."

Horace Greeley says : "The proper cure for a guerilla is hemp, looped over the first tree, guerilla pendant." The following also is from that infamous sheet, the New York Tribune : " There is much excitement in Nashville, and there is great fear of a rebel attack on that city. At the Murfreesboro' fight $30,000 worth of army stores were lost on our side. The Pennsylvania 7th lost 200 men—only three or four of their officers escaped. *The rebel loss is said to be greater than ours.*" The latter is what the Yankees always record. In all their reports of battles they wind up by saying, " the rebel loss is said to be greater than ours." In the case above referred to, a more disgraceful lie was never recorded even by a Yankee.

The Northern papers stated a week ago, and we were assured, that a general exchange of prisoners had been agreed upon by the two governments. In yesterday's Tribune I find the following: " We are assured that the report of an agreement for a general exchange of prisoners is premature. Yet it is thought that both sides will favor some immediate arrangement." The bill for the admission of the " State of Western Virginia," after a long discussion, was yesterday adopted by a vote of 23 to 17 In the House the Ways and Means Committee reported the Miscellaneous Appropriation Bill, with the donation to Gales & Seaton *stricken out.* The Yankee Congress adjourned to-day

July 17th. From the Baltimore *Sun,* of July 12th, I extract : " A Washington paper states that the government has agreed upon a general exchange of prisoners of war, and that arrangements will speedily be made for the sending South of the prisoners now held on the seaboard. All the prisoners confined at New York were taken on board a steamer yesterday." A western correspondent of a Yankee paper, under date of Vicksburg, July 7th, says: " General Hindman is reported to be at Little Rock with a large force. He has with him a million dollars in gold and silver, which he obtained ' by the authority of the sword' from the banks in Memphis. He is disliked by his troops for his oppressiveness and tyranny. His last order was for the impressment of every man in Arkansas capable of bearing arms. This, of course, has created a great deal of indignation among the people, and has made many enemies to the cause of Secession. Hindman, as a General, is the same swaggering bombast that he was as a Congressman. In his own town of Helena he is despised worse than the meanest and most contemptible citizen. He took advantage of the temporary insanity of the people to put himself in a position that would not have been assigned him at any time since. His debut in the rebellion was made at the head of the " Hindman Legion," which he raised immediately after his return from Washington City, after the secession of his gallant State."

" Simon Cohen was arrested in Baltimore on Monday, by officer

Scott, charged with displaying a Secession flag at his store, No. 185 Gay street. He was held for the action of the provost marshal. Also, Leonard Strikpon spent the day at a lager beer saloon on the Belair Road, and imbibed somewhat freely, so much so, that he lost his senses, and hurrahed for Jeff. Davis. Officer Smith took him into custody, and Justice Spicer sent him to jail in default of bail to keep the peace."—*Baltimore News Sheet.*

Colonel Hanson, of Kentucky, was to-day transferred to Fort Warren, according to his own request.

July 18*th.* Anniversary of the battle at Bull Run. The prisoners seem in fine spirits to-day in recollection of our victory a year' ago, though it's hard to be cheerful in a room so dull as the one in which we are confined! There is nothing in it that can awaken the mind or call up a sentiment of solace! "The dawning of morn, the day-light sinking," generally furnishes us the same monotony! But the moody silence our thoughts shed over us in this comfortless confinement is often broken by the cheerful songs of Lieutenant S., who forces us to ask ourselves,

> " Why, soldiers, why
> Should we be melancholy, boys?"

The daily promises of "Old Gip," that Jackson's men shall be paroled in a few days, are not believed; yet, with this unbelief is blended a ray of hope, and for one I say, "for God's sake destroy not the hopes that man holds out to me ; upon them I live." Dr. Reid says if we cannot imbibe the spirit, it is often profitable to put on the appearance of cheerfulness. "By *seeming* gay, we grow to what we seem."

Thousands of dollars worth of clothing have been sent to the Confederate prisoners by Secessionists, and very little do they get. "Old Gip" refuses to give it to many who are in a destitute condition, but he makes the impression outside, that all clothing sent to us by Secession friends is given to us. A box was sent to Captain R. (a prisoner) with clothing in it, to distribute among the destitute prisoners, but Gibson refused to allow him. The clothing is given to Yankee soldiers. The Dutch Captain *Mtowlowski* paid us a visit to-day He is a florid, fat, happy-looking, short fellow, with legs so thick, that they very much resemble an elephant's. His face is large and rosy, and its general expression a mixture of good humor and inexhaustible drollery He wears a moustache *a la militaire.* On the whole, he presents the appearance of a migratory lager beer keg. He would be muscular, had not lager beer enervated his strong build, by placing a superabundance of useless fat where muscle ought to be. The Captain says that he was a prisoner in Europe, and that our fare is a paradise to what his was, which is very hard to believe.

To-day my thoughts have turned to my early friends—those

who have been weighed in the balance and found not wanting.
The thoughts of early friendship ! what a world of tender memory they suggest.   For what are all our later successes in life,
however bright our fortunes, compared with the early triumphs
of boyish days ?   Where, among the jealous rivalry of some, the
cold and half-wrung praise of others, the selfish and unsympa-
thizing regard of all, shall we find anything to repay us for the
swelling exstacy of our young hearts, as we pledged ourselves to
each other in prosperity or adversity in the noble bonds of friendship ?   Some moments we have which half seem to realize our
early dreams of ambition, and rouse the spirit within us.   But
what were all compared to our boyish glories—to the little world
of sympathy and love our early friendships teemed with as we
pledged ourselves to each other ?   No, the world has no requi-
tal for this !   It is like a bright day, which, as its glories gild the
east, display before us a whole world of beauty and promise.
Then our hopes have not withered—false friendships have not
scathed—cold, selfish interest has not yet hardened our hearts
or dried up our affections, and we are indeed happy ; but equally, like the burst of morning, it is short-lived and fleeting, and
equally does it pass away, never to return.

July 19*th.*   My thoughts this morning have been engrossed
upon the subject of being exchanged or paroled—on being
again among congenial friends in the "Old Dominion !"   But
I shall no longer allow my fortune or lot to be the sport of my
temperament.   I shall not give way to that April-day frame of
mind which is ever the jest and scoff of those hardier and
sterner natures, who, if never overjoyed by success, are never
much depressed by failure ; for the glimpses of sunshine the
world has afforded me, fleeting and passing enough, in all con-
science, I am not so ungrateful as to repine, because it was not
permanent.   On the other hand, I am thankful for those bright
hours, which, if nothing more, are, at least, delightful souve-
nirs.   They form the golden thread in the tangled web of our
existence, ever appearing amid the darker surface around, and
throwing a fair halo of brilliancy on what—without it—were
cold, bleak and barren.

Lieutenant ———, since he has been in prison here, wrote to
his cousin at York, Pennsylvania, a friendly letter, and received
the following reply :—"Cousin, I can hardly call you dear
cousin, for were I in the Union army you might have shot me
if you would have had the chance, which I do think you would
do if you get the chance ; so as it is your thoughts to kill all
Northern men that you can, relation or not, and which I do
think it is a shame for you to do, being as all your relations

lives in the North, and are all Union people, so far as I know of, which place I seen yesterday you was born in twenty years ago, and eighty years ago your grand father fought for the glorious country, and now you want to turn right around to drive it to nothing at the point of the bayonet, which I do think that you are doing wrong. Had I a hold of you I know I would make you git—if you was pressed into it I can forgive you, but if you fight against this country free-hearted I can't forgive you, and don't fear you neither. It is right that they have taken you a prisoner, and I hope they will deal with you as they ought, being as they have you, and all such friends and relations as I have in the rebel army, if there are more of them. I hope in some future day you may see how wrong you have done to trample down that banner which waves over once so glorious a country as this. Now, as a rebel, you want to destroy it. Shame on you as a Christian, as you wanted to be in days gone by. I still thought you had more respect for this country than you show for up to this time. Think of this letter whenever you write to me—think that you are writing to a Union cousin, *which has more sense in his big toe than you have in your head.* For me to come to see you is impossible for me to do. If you was there, and I knowed you was doing write, I might come, but so I cannot; and you must think hard of me for writing such a letter to you, for I have no sympathy for a man that will do such a villanous act as you have done to this country. If you had any thoughts for yourself and your relations you might have got out of that rascally rebel army as well as you have got into it. Your relations that you enquire about are all well. If I had Jeff Davis, and you together, I would hang both of you. So now you can do as you please ; you can write, or leave it alone ; but that is what I think of you. If you write, tell me where your father is.

J. S. B."

This is the Lieutenant's rejoinder :

" Cousin J., this is a wicked world, and there are many strange people and funny things in it. Your recent letter might be classed among the latter, if it were possible for a thing to be curious, without possessing some interest. And now, for yourself, you might be a strange man if you were not precisely like all the rest of the cowards, " Full of sound and fury, and doing nothing. Why are you not in the army battling for that glorious country which you charge your rebel cousin with attempting to destroy Your President wants men, and just such laggards as yourself will compel a draft upon the whole people before your army is complete. 'Tis nice talk and little labor to say pretty things about the cause in which you pretend to be heartily enlisted with your *pen ;* but before all the rebels are destroyed, you may discover that many such windy patriots as yourself will be required to lay aside the pen, and buckle on the sword. The draft which will soon be resorted to in your State may bring you into the field, and the fates of war may place you in the hands of my government. Then, if you will let me hear from you, I will teach you a Christian's duty ; and while you have scoffed at my calamity, I will endeavor to alleviate your suffering, not because you happen to be my cousin, but for the sake of humanity. Before you write to me again, I would have you leave off such vulgar notions as you now entertain of me and my brother rebels. After nine days, even, a puppy's eyes are opened. May not cousin Josiah hope for light ?"

Sunday, July 20th. It is said that the small pox has broken out in the barracks. There is certainly a case of small pox at the upper part of the island, whither he has been taken from the barracks.

The most insidious schemes are constantly resorted to by the Yankees to lead men to take the oath of allegiance. Their present condition is placed before them in colors as dark as they are ; and in contrast a most captivating picture of happy freedom, in flowers of rhetoric, is presented to them, provided they throw Secession to the winds, and assume the garb of " the Union, the Constitution and the laws." Gold is also offered them as an inducement to become traitors. Very few, comparatively, have been thus seduced to treason, and those few have been mostly of Northern birth, or else outcasts from society at home, who joined the army not from principle but from necessity. On the contrary, to the large majority of the prisoners these seductive devices are as the storm to the oak, which, though it may scatter the leaves, and snap the smaller branches, serves but to rivet the roots, and to harden and condense the fibres of the tree.

Last night there was great excitement in the garrison on account of the attempt of prisoners to escape. Several companies were called out, and great noise prevailed, while getting the men into line of battle. Cannon was turned on the barracks. Several prisoners, I understand, escaped.

July 21st. Anniversary of the battle of Manassas ! The disturbance last night has been denominated the " Pea Patch battle." Mysterious as it may seem, Captain S. succeeded to-day in getting a bottle of whiskey, to the astonishment no less than the delight of our mess. A quart of whiskey ! How charming to chase away dull care ! The Captain brought it into the room, with a commingled air of joy and self congratulation, as he exhibited the evidence of his prowess, while he repeated the lines :

"How sad and short were this life's dull day,
Were it not brightened with pleasure,
I then, for my part, will sport it away
In friendship, love, and of folly a measure."

Lieutenant D. said if he meant by folly the whiskey, he heartily endorsed the sentiment, and with a general exchange of wit, the bottle was soon discussed among so many.

A Baltimore paper states that "no little excitement was created in Baltimore yesterday by the public display of a "Secesh rag" by Miss Mattie Gilpin, daughter of John Gilpin, of Elkton, Cecil county. Miss Gilpin was first observed passing from the President street depot in company with her sister, and in addition to the flag, which is about twenty inches in length, she wore a large Secesh rosette on the bosom of her dress. Two policemen followed them some distance, and finally took both in custody, conducting them to Marshal Van Nastrand's office. A warrant was issued by Justice Hess, and after a long conversation with the Marshal, in which Miss Gilpin manifested no regret at the part she was playing, she was released on security to await the action of the grand jury on the charge of violating the treason act of the recent General Assembly of this State by displaying a Secession flag with the view of exciting seditious feelings." The most important news to-day is, that Major General Halleck has been called to Washington, and put in chief command of all the armies of the Union. The tone of the papers, however, indicate that this does not affect Generals McClellan and Pope, who retain their present position.

The Tribune says : " General Pope's advance, upon reaching Gordonsville, destroyed all the railway material at hand. As a great portion of the rebel supplies come by this route, the blow to them will be a serious one." The same paper says : " The Richmond papers are much disturbed at the consolidation of the army of Virginia. Pope is reckoned a fighting General—hence their trouble." General Pope has ordered his troops to subsist on the enemy, but adds that any man who is loyal from the date of the seizure of his property shall be paid. Dates from Fortress Monroe, to Wednesday last, give no news from McClellan's army. " Cynthana, Kentucky, has been captured by the rebels under Morgan." The difficulty about the exchange of prisoners seems to be about settled, if it be true, as reported in the papers, that General Dix had a satisfactory interview with Gene-

8

ral Hill, and then went up the James river to have an interview
with General Lee to that end. The trouble all along has been
that the Yankees have been *fools* enough to suppose that they
might capture some of the leaders of our cause, and have the
pleasure of hanging them, or exercising their malice in some
other way, and they know that the Confederate Government will
not exchange, except in prospective or upon a cartel, that will
occasion no trouble hereafter, by adopting the principle of the
war of 1812. It is all a humbug about General Buckner standing in the way of exchange, for he has been treated as a *prisoner
of war;* and what objection, in a civilized warfare, can they
have to exchange him with the other prisoners of war?

July 22*d.* A Pennsylvania soldier writes from Tuscumbia,
Alabama, to the Philadelphia " Evening Bulletin :" " The people are, of course, very extensive slaveholders, few of them own-
ing less than eighty slaves. Of course they are, without exception, the rankest kind of Secessionists, and bestow upon us looks
anything but affectionate as we pass along. One old rebel, in
whose clover meadow we encamped on our last day's march,
perfectly raved at the damned Yankees. His slaves were out in
the cornfield when we came, and he ordered them in, and told
them he would whip them within an inch of their lives if they
attempted to escape."

The noise and bombast of the Yankee editors over victories,
large or small, or oftener over defeats, (for they always have
some excuse other than cowardice,) is most remarkable and
illaudable. For instance, General Jackson's army advanced
upon Front Royal, and the first Maryland and Wheat's battalion on our side took prisoners, all but fifteen of the first Maryland and the Vermont cavalry on the Yankee side. This the
Yankee papers most plausibly distorted into a Confederate defeat, as it " placed Jackson in a position from which he cannot
escape." The sequel has proved that Jackson not only escaped,
but whipped Banks most completely at Winchester, Fremont at
Port Republic, and McDowell and Shields at Cross Keyes. The
Yankees are ever bragging about their grand army—the number of their men. While boasting what they are going to do in
one breath with this " grand army," with the next, they call for
volunteers.

The Wheeling Intelligencer says : " All the merchants in the
city, except one, have taken the oath of allegiance. One physician, enjoying a large practice, gave it up, rather than take
the oath." Nearly all the Virginia merchants had left before
the Yankees had the power to offer the insult. The physician,
who would not take the oath of allegiance, is Dr. Hughes,

The merchants, who did take it, had the alternative of taking the oath or being imprisoned, and lose all their property. It is hard for a man to work all his life, and then to give up all and go to prison, leaving his family destitute. The merchants took the oath *under protest*. The abolition editor does not state this however, for the object of the Yankees is to deceive, and such a mark of magnanimity would not be in accordance with their character. Nearly all the regiments which the bogus Pierpont government call Virginia regiments, are filled with Ohio Abolitionists.

July 24th. A lady, in Washington city, sent me the following by the "Underground mail carrier," saying she "heartily endorsed the words:"

REBELS

BY A. P. T.

Rebels! 'tis a ho'y name!
The name our fathers bore
When battling in the cause of right,
In the dark days of yore.

Rebels! 'tis our family name!
Our father—Washington—
Was the arch-Rebel in the fight,
And gives the name to us, a right
Of father unto son.

Rebels! 'tis our given name!
Our mother—Liberty—
Received the title with her fame
In days of grief, and fear and shame,
When at her breast were we.

Rebels! 'tis our sealed name!
A baptism of blood.
The war-cry and the dire of strife,
The fearful contest, life for life,
The mingled crimson blood.

Rebels! 'tis a patriot name!
In struggles it was given;
We bore it then, when tyrants raved,
And thro' their curses 'twas engraved
On the Dooms-day Book of Heaven.

Rebels! 'tis our fighting name!
For peace rolls o'er the land,
Until they speak of craven woe,
Until our rights receive a blow
From foe's or brother's hand.

Rebels! 'tis our dying name!
For although life is dear,
Yet freemen born, and freemen bred,
We'd rather lie as freemen dead,
Then live in slavish fear.

Then call us Rebels if you will,
We'll glory in the name;
For bending under unjust laws,
And swearing faith to un unjust cause,
We count a greater shame.

"A perfect love of a man" is Parson Brownlow. The Louisville Journal says : "He has repeatedly assured us that he never swore an oath, never played a card, never took a drink of liquor, never went to the theatre, never attended a horse-race, never told a lie, never broke the Sabbath, never voted the Democratic ticket, never wore whiskers, and never kissed any woman but his wife. He is a black-hearted traitor, besides being an unprincipled liar.

A Western editor says his paper is located immediately over a *recruiting* office, and that the fifing and drumming "drives everything out of his head." What a scampering there must be over his shirt collar !

All the Yankees talk about is "the Union and its laws." Of all injustice, that is the greatest which goes under the name of law ; and of all sorts of tyranny, the forcing of the letter of the law against the equity is the most insupportable.

Many Yankee soldiers have assured me that they entered the army while intoxicated with drink, being victims of the wiles of those who do not scruple to do anything in their mad efforts to conquer the South. Wrong being at the root of their great armies, has caused them so often to bite the dust before inferior numbers :

> "Although the ear be deaf, and will not hear,
> There is a voice in conscience which appeals
> Unto the heart of guilt.   A still, small voice,
> Which, like the mountain streamlet, wears its way
> Over the hardest rock."

The small armies of the Confederates have the advantage of *right* on their side, and

> "How weak an army can strike a giant's blow;
> When Providence directs it."   *   *

July 25th.   Gold to-day is a peg higher, closing at 120½, with a sharp demand for export.   Flour, wheat and corn, following the law of attraction, are "up" too.   Inflation is the order of the day, and under the exhilarating influence of plenty of paper money, nobody appears to dream of the possibility that the bubble is ever going to burst.   I glean the following from Northern papers : The news from Louisville, Kentucky, concerning Morgan's movements is, that between Crab Orchard and London he destroyed several wagons of a Federal train destined for General Morgan's command at Cumberland Gap.   Of course the wagons, whose number is indefinitely stated, were not empty ones, but whether they contained commissary stores, or material of war, is not mentioned.   The "Courier" and "Eugene," whilst ascending Green River, Kentucky, with troops, were fired into by a party of cavalry. At McAllister's landing, two miles beyond Newburg, Indiana, the steamer Commercial was also attacked in a similar manner ; whilst at Randolph, Missouri, the Belle, on her way from Memphis to St. Louis, was likewise fired upon. "The result," we are told, "was unknown." At Hudson, Missouri, Porter's guerrillas were attacked and routed by a detachment of Federal cavalry under Colonel McNeill. The Federal loss is set down at fifteen killed and thirty wounded. The guerrilla loss is said to be much heavier. There was renewed excitement at Nashville, Tennessee, on Monday evening last—the Federal pickets on the Lebanon having been captured by the guerrillas under Colonel Forrest, who was reported to be in force within five miles of the city. The Confederates have also broken up the railway communication between Corinth and Tuscumbia. As the Tennessee river is no longer navigable, in consequence of the low stage of water, great difficulty, it is said, will be experienced in providing with adequate supplies those portions of Buell's army which are at or near Tuscumbia.

We know but little concerning the present condition of the army now encamped under cover of the gunboats on the James river, beyond what is furnished by the correspondents of Northern journals. From these sources, however, we learn that the furlough fever has somewhat abated, that many of those who contemplated asking for leave of absence have concluded to remain, but that many other officers, surfeited with war and its horrors, have sent in their resignations, and "want to go home." The Confederates are reported to be in considerable force on both sides of the James river, from four to eight miles below the mouth of the Chickahominy, whilst above, at Turkey Island Bend, Curl's Neck, and at Dutch Gap, they are constructing large and massive batteries. On several occasions the gun boats have driven them from their work, but it was resumed again as soon as the boats retired, and the batteries are now supposed to be "fully prepared, equipped, and ready for future action." It is not surprising, then, that it should be rumored "that the troops would receive orders, in the course of a few days, to evacuate their present position," where they suffer terribly for want of pure and wholesome water, and are weakened down with diarrhœa and dysentery. It seems scarcely probable, however, that McClellan will abandon the "secure" position he has already sacrificed so much to attain. The report to that effect is, nevertheless, gravely announced by the correspondent of the Philadelphia Enquirer, and is reproduced, without comment, in the New York papers. The War Department has issued an order authorizing the military commanders within the States of **Virginia**, South Carolina, Georgia, Alabama, Mississippi, Louisiana, Texas and Arkansas, to seize any real or personal property which may be necessary or convenient for their respective commands, and also to destroy property for military purposes. It is further ordered that the negroes within and from the above States shall be employed as laborers for military purposes, giving them reasonable compensation for their services, and that a record shall be kept, showing from whom the property and persons are taken, as a basis upon which compensation can be made in proper cases.

Saturday, July 26th. The papers say that McClellan remains quiet, while his officers are resigning as fast as they can. He may fly from our brave soldiers, and seek shelter under his gunboats, but he cannot flee from the retributive justice of heaven, let him go where he may :

> " In vain he flies—the furies still pursue.
> Avenging justice on the murderer's track
> Follows to claim her due."

It is with a loathing, sickening sensation, similar to that with which men regard the bloated toad or slimy reptile, that I view the Yankee officials who come round daily, often with no other object but to tantalize the prisoners. The idea that their treasonable invasion of the just rights of the South has placed me in my present position, sends the warm blood rushing to my heart and brain—my shattered nerves resume their elasticity, and feel as if they were suddenly transformed to steel. More than once I have clenched my hands with nervous impatience, till the nails almost cut the flesh, for the Yankees, from their very nature, seem to feel an almost inhuman joy in contemplating our imprisonment ; and what is more calculated to vex ? We were allowed to go a swimming this evening. Saw two young ladies—nearer than I have seen a lady for two months, for they passed directly by us. They were, indeed, fair and good-looking, but as they did not condescend to notice me :

> " Why should I, wasting in despair,
> Die because a woman's fair;
> What care I how fair she be,
> If she be not fair to me."

It was told us on Friday that we would certainly be sent to Dixie to-day, but to-day they say we are not to go until Monday. I believe the sole delight of the Yankee authorities here is to tantalize us as much as they can. I read somewhere that the word tantalize thus originated—a man named Tantalus had been found guilty of a crime in Germany, and as a punishment for the same he was denied water for a certain length of time, although water, by machinery, passed nearer every moment to his parched lips—every moment the cooling draught suddenly swept by him in pipes, and became more and more close to his mouth, but yet never near enough for him to quench his thirst. Afterwards whenever a man had expectations of a flattering nature held out to him and was frustrated, he was said to be tantalized. Truly, the Yankees are fond of tantalizing—they like to deceive and tyrannize over those in their power. All cowards are prone to do the same.

On the 15th of July, Sergeant J. J Cox, first battalion Louisiana volunteers, and John A. Toole, 9th Virginia cavalry, made their escape from Fort Delaware under the following circumstances: At 8 o'clock, P M., when the sergeants were calling the roll in the enclosure, they squeezed out of the apertures left for the passage of air throughout the quarters, and concealed themselves in the long grass outside the barracks. They now had about ten paces to crawl in order to reach the path on which the sentry walked, and they passed this point in safety and unobserved by the sentinel, with their knives between their teeth, ready to use at any moment. They then crossed the moat and embankment in safety. It was now seventy-five yards to the river. On the way there they discovered a board on which they tied their clothes. As they were about to get into the water, they saw a boat full (as they supposed) of soldiers rowing towards the shore, and in about ten minutes another came. This delayed them an hour, when they leaped into the water, and swam half way across the river. Here a government transport passed so close to them that they could discern every rope on board. Having eluded this boat they had no further trouble, and reached the shore between Delaware City and New Castle on the marsh, after being five or six hours in the water, and having swam a distance of three and a half miles on a board ! They remained on the marsh until the night of the 16th, when they started on their journey South—passed the town of St. George, Delaware, the same night. They went to Baltimore and Washington to look round, and from the latter they made their way to Dixie, easy enough, in the character of stock buyers.

July 28th. This day has been spent in reading the "life of Washington," loaned me by a fellow-prisoner. The war for independence has always been considered the heroic age in American history, and while many despaired of peace ever again smiling upon the land, Washington placed his confidence in God, and overcame all difficulties. In September, 1775, Washington wrote in relation to a proposed attack upon the enemy at Boston and Roxbury : "The success of such an enterprise, I well know, *depends on the all-wise disposer of events,* and is not within the reach of human wisdom to foretell the result

January, 1776, he wrote : "For more than two months I have scarcely emerged from one difficulty before I have plunged into another. How it will end God in his great goodness will direct." Those who fight the battles of a country may derive their loftiest inspirations from trust in providence. In July, 1775, Washington said in an order to the troops : "The fate of unborn millions will now depend, under God, on the courage and conduct of this army. Let us rely upon the goodness of the cause, and the aid of the Supreme Being, in whose hands victory is."

July 29th, 30th and 31st. Nothing of interest enough to record has transpired during the past three days, unless it be the arrival of transport boats to convey us to "Dixie," which latter is the only evidence to our minds that we are really to be exchanged, for we have ceased to believe the Yankees any longer. And I might add, the general happiness manifested by the prisoners in anticipation of once more realizing that freedom which allows one to move about at pleasure, and untrammelled by a sentinel at every step. No one can entertain an adequate idea of what liberty is, until he has been confined in a Yankee prison, and then he will understand both liberty and tyranny.

August 1st. About three thousand Confederates were put on board boats to-day, and started for the South—landed at "Aiken's Landing," August 5th.

My prison experience has taught me that the Yankees are one grand bundle of lies and inconsistencies. The newspapers, particularly, have begun, and kept up, a wholsale system of lying, under the military censorship and direction of the Secretary of War. In spite of their disclaimers to the contrary, their own acts and words betray their purpose to steal all the negroes they can. It is true that some have pleaded, and are now pleading for peace under the old government, offering the South all she ever had, and claiming nothing that is not common to all. But this is simply because they have seen the folly of their undertaking, and would like now to slip out of the difficulty, especially since they believe they have about as many slaves as they will probably get. But those who are now causing all the bloodshed around us, will, if they persist, find the bounds of slavery yet spread beyond limits heretofore held. The Confederate Government, however, is fighting for *Constitutional Liberty*—the liberty of our forefathers against all things, and nothing but annihilation can prevent them from upholding it ; and to the Yankees it may be said :

you undertake is dangerous ;
have named uncertain ;
unsorted ;
ole plot too light for the counterpoise of so great an opposition."

www.ingramcontent.com/pod-product-compliance
Lightning Source LLC
Chambersburg PA
CBHW021631270326
41931CB00008B/974